MASTERING CANDLE MAGIC

PATRICIA TELESCO

MASTERING CANDLE MAGIC

ADVANCED SPELLS AND CHARMS FOR EVERY RITE

Chicago, IL

Paperback ISBN: 978-1-959883-51-7
Hardcover ISBN: 978-1-959883-88-3
Library of Congress Control Number on file.

Cover design by Blake Malliway.
Edited by Kumari Pacheco.
Typesetting by Mads Oliver.

Published by:
Crossed Crow Books, LLC
6934 N Glenwood Ave, Suite C
Chicago, IL 60626
www.crossedcrowbooks.com

Printed in the United States of America.

CONTENTS

INTRODUCTION

Thousands of candles can be lighted from a single candle,
and the life of the candle will not be shortened.
Happiness never decreases by being shared.
—Buddha

I would go one step further to say that candlelight, when shared, *encourages* happiness and contentment. There is a special ambiance and magic in the glow of a candle—and our ancestors recognized it. As early as their invention, human beings were lighting some form of candle to banish the darkness of night and the darkness of Spirit that often surrounded them in a harsh world.

While our lives are not as difficult as theirs, they are certainly more complex. We also need that hopeful light—the glow and happiness that comes from a single taper lit with thoughtful intention. Thus, Candle Magic remains one of the oldest, most widely practiced, and most deeply respected methods in the metaphysical world. *Mastering Candle Magic* builds on the foundation established by our ancestors and contemporaries alike. Before the word *mastering* puts you off, however, let me explain that in the pages of this book, this term denotes and promotes an attitude, outlook, and approach more than anything else. If we are walking our walk every moment of every day, our lives become an act of worship. From here, all else is simply icing on that proverbial cake. (And in this case, we get the candles too!)

Some of you might be thinking that Candle Magic is, by its very definition, *low magic*—magic of the common people practiced in simple, functional, and sublime ways. You would be correct! We need not reinvent the wheel here. If the method isn't broken, why fix it? There is no way that I (or any author) could make Candle Magic more approachable and adaptable than it is already. Instead, *Mastering Candle Magic* strives to give you sound constructs and fresh ideas for using traditional techniques in new, meaningful ways, specifically in combination with some of the emerging components and tools that technology provides for us.

In my previous works on Candle Magic, we discussed using candles in specific settings—for divination, rituals, spellcraft, feng shui, charms, prayers, meditations, and astrology. Now we're going to take a slightly different approach and look at applying this wonderfully accessible method to everyday needs and goals. Are you tired of being in a dead-end job? Are you looking for coven mates that share your magical vision? Do you want to build a spiritual kinship with those who make you feel wholly at home? Do you long for intimate, lasting companionship? All of these things—and many more—can be accomplished through the creative, willful, and determined application of Candle Magic.

But don't stop there. Include one other very important aspiration: your growth as a magical person. It's been said that we are spiritual beings having a human experience—I believe that statement is true. In that context, each of us is a candle in our own right. Your soul is the candle's eternal wick; your heart, its flame. Your mind and your desire to learn are the air that gives it life, and your body is the wax. By understanding this symbolism, you can burn ever more brightly and come closer to fulfilling your quest for enlightenment.

In that same vein, *Mastering Candle Magic* discusses the symbolic value of candles when connecting with our own souls—and with Spirit on an intimate level. It also shares ideas for creating your own candlelight spells (or adapting those you find in this or any other book) so that they're truly meaningful. By so doing, this book becomes a candle grimoire in every sense of the word, one to which you can turn again and again for constructs or inspiration.

So, how does all this make our candle magic efforts advanced? Perhaps *advanced* is a poor choice of words. It's certainly no more complex, time-consuming, or difficult than before. Rather, the idea here is to master our practices and art so that they live outside the proverbial box. Advance them with your sincerity, intensity, and determination. Advance them based on your patience, creativity, and sensitivity. Candle Magic, like any spiritual method, advances as far and as fast as you allow in your own spirit!

Let there be a light in the darkness.
Let our magic shine.
We put flame to wick,
And together, in the warmth of the candle's glow,
We begin...

PART I
The Next Step

*Acquaintance without patience is like a
candle with no light.*

—Iranian proverb

CHAPTER ONE
BUILDING THE BASICS

A candle loses nothing by lighting another candle.
—Father James Keller

The Latin root word for *advance* means "to promote," "bring to the forefront," "furnish to others," "enhance (or improve)," and "move forward." These definitions give us a fine place to start our journey through *Mastering Candle Magic*. As mentioned in the introduction, *advanced* in this setting doesn't necessarily mean "more complex"—only a little more creative, insightful, and responsible.

Mastering Candle Magic promotes this ancient art by further establishing it as an accepted and adored metaphysical method, as well as a spiritual expression that has plenty of room for personalization and growth. Candle Magic came out of the warm and wise traditions of everyday folk. In contrast to the harshness of modern lighting, candles speak to us of less chaotic times. Their glow is comforting and hopeful, like the dawn. The process underpinning nearly all Candle Magic efforts is reasonably straightforward, and better still is the availability of its media. This combination attracted our ancestors, and today, folks find Candle Magic just as appealing!

Again, I am not one to recreate the wheel when the one I have works just fine. However, in order to roll forward the wheel of progression, I strongly advocate that we take the best of what we have from Candle Magic's history and put our own spin on it. Like leaving your fingerprint on a glass, by taking the time to experiment and play with your media (namely candles), you impress them with your energy signature. This, in turn, leads to wholly unique and meaningful results (i.e., your personal *spin* on the energy).

In terms of the root definition of "bring to the forefront," I want to stress that while Candle Magic is a simple art form, it can have sublime beauty. We need to raise the bar in how we perceive this ancient practice and not let the natural ease of the processes fool us into thinking that Candle Magic is any less powerful or practicable. The notion that fanciness makes for better outcomes is a very worldly one. Spiritually speaking, simplicity does not equate to wimpy results. Our ancestors were not foolish; if a process didn't yield results, they would stop using it. Simplicity is part of what endears Candle Magic to the heart of the most adept spiritual seekers. In our busy world, simple and functional is good!

Beyond this, magic has always been about creating changes. Because we face environments daily where transformations are needed or desired, our magical methods need to be *brought to the forefront* of everyday life. Candles represent a beautiful way to achieve this goal without necessarily invoking images of Witches in pointy hats. (I mean, how many people do you know personally who have candles in their house and do not practice magic?) This is very important for those practitioners who cannot—because of personal circumstances—be wholly out of their proverbial broom closet.

The whole purpose behind *Mastering Candle Magic* is one of exploring ways to add in, personalize, or enhance your candle-lighting efforts for any ritual, spell, charm, meditation, or other metaphysical process. The ideas I'm presenting here are ones I've tried with a reasonable amount of success, but they're not being doled out as dogma. As always, please trust in that small voice within to know what works best for you. It may seem obvious, but it's a very important reminder, especially for newer practitioners who may feel a little uncertain. You truly do have the power to make and change your reality, but that magic only works if you trust your heart.

Speaking of trusting and trying—Candle Magic is among the most adaptable of all the Wise Crafts, as proven by the experimentation process you'll try out later in this book. Its components are easily obtained and inexpensive. (The frugal, time-challenged Kitchen Witch in me sees this as the best of all worlds!) You shouldn't have to go much further than your pantry or supermarket shelf to find the ingredients for every activity listed herein. And when you can't find the exact items, there are ideas for substitution included in each section. Which brings me to my next topic: how to adapt the candlelight spells you find in this or other books.

Adapting and Personalizing Prefabricated Candle Magic Spells

The best candle is understanding.
—Welsh proverb

While it is certainly much easier on your schedule to use a prefabricated spell, the results aren't always as satisfying, especially if something seems amiss in the initial perusal. One step toward adeptness is being able to recognize when a process (or its components) isn't quite right for your vision and path. This section will provide some guidelines on how to adapt and personalize candlelight spells so that they manifest in the most successful and fulfilling way possible.

First, ask yourself: What's the problem with this spell? Is it the components, the symbolism, the wording, the focus?

If the components are the issue—either because you don't have the ones recommended or you don't want to work with those items—that's one of the easiest things to fix. For example, if you don't have the suggested aromatic oil, use a good correspondence list (such as the one provided in Appendix B) to find another appropriate one. Say you're fresh out of rose oil with which to anoint your candle in a love spell. You could use lavender, jasmine, vanilla, or violet (among many others) instead. Or, if you happen to have rosewater in your pantry, that'd do the trick too!

What about components that modern practitioners no longer use or those with which they may be unfamiliar? The same type of substitution holds true. It is, however, important that you fully understand the contextual purpose of the ingredient. If, for example, a spell calls for dabbing the bottom of the candle with Treacle, the natural reaction of most folk would be, "What the heck is Treacle?" There's nothing wrong with Treacle, even if it sounds funny; it's actually just the old name for molasses, an excellent component for symbolizing the desire to hold fast to an idea or goal. In this case, it was just a matter of doing a little research to fully appreciate the meaning of the original spell rather than actually needing to substitute anything. Don't have molasses? How about glue or bubble gum?

This example brings me to an important point that cannot be stressed enough no matter how advanced the practitioner or the process: meaningfulness is nothing less than essential in magic. Sure, it might be a little time-consuming to discern the meanings of oddly spelled, older words. But if you don't understand what you're supposed to use and why, you won't be able to find a suitable substitute that will make the spell actually *work* for you. Without that mental connection to the process or symbols, your spell simply won't produce the necessary energy.

Similarly (and this may sound a bit militant), if you're going through the motions just to impress someone, stop right now! Magic is between you and Spirit, you and your heart. If you cross over personal ideals or taboos in your process, any stray magic that's created is likely to go awry anyway.

Speaking of taboos, there are a lot of old spells that include ingredients that are unacceptable by modern standards. For example, many of the ancient grimoires include spells that call for blood because it was considered a very personal and very powerful component. Now, in our health-conscious day and age, avoiding that ingredient is sensible. Look instead to a couple of alternatives such as saliva or, if wishing for a color correspondence, tomato juice. The saliva compares well to blood as a personal body fluid; the tomato juice corresponds in texture and color.

The important thing in all cases of adaptation is that you maintain continuity of the symbolic value. So, if you have issues with the symbols used in a spell, change them, but make sure your changes make sense. Let's say the spell's instructions call for carving an upward-pointing arrow to represent an increase of energy. You, however, prefer the mathematical sign for *greater than* (>). The solution is simple. Carve the mathematical sign into the candle instead. The carving still maintains the basic value of all parts of the spell, but it also means more to you when you look at it.

Next, we'll want to consider the wording. Let's face it: very few of today's practitioners are comfortable with Shakespearean-style prose. Read over any verbal components and say them out loud. Does anything stick on your tongue or feel completely foreign? Those are the words and phrases you should seriously consider changing. Focus is everything in spellcraft, and if you're worrying over your words, you'll have less energy to give.

The same applies to any spells that include words from foreign languages. I highly suggest you either have a working knowledge of that language—or have access to someone who can teach you the correct pronunciation—before using any such incantation. Incorrect inflection, tone, or pronunciation can dramatically change the meanings of some foreign words and phrases. Unless you enjoy completely uncontrolled surprises in your spellcraft, know what you're saying and how to say it, or substitute words from your native tongue.

This brings up a good point for readers for whom English is a second language. If you are more comfortable using Spanish, French, or German, translate your spells into that language. Our minds react to language in very specific ways; words do, indeed, have power. There is absolutely no reason *not* to work with the linguistic construct with which you're familiar— you'll only have greater understanding.

What about the spell's focus? I know that sounds odd, but I've read some very well-constructed ancient spells that I would *never* consider using for their intended purposes. For example, one spell says to put a nail in the footprint of an enemy to cause them harm (probably somewhat similar to using a poppet). While the White Witch in me recoils at such a dark deed, the symbolic value really grabs my attention. To adapt this concept to Candle Magic, I'd suggest pushing a nail through a candle while reciting an incantation, then letting the candle burn to that point (akin to having an "X" that marks the spot where the magic really takes flight).

Useful Ideas for Spell Adaptation and Creation

+ Rather than using one candle, use several
  arranged in a symbolic pattern.

+ Make Candle Magic a group effort, with each
  person bringing and lighting a significant candle.

+ Move with a candle through a pattern (literally
  putting your magic into action), or move other items
  around the candle to create a pattern of power.

+ As you light the candle, remember your purpose.
  As you put it out, understand that while this signals
  closure for the spell, the energy keeps moving.

+ Turn candles clockwise in their base a symbolic
  number of times to generate positive "spin";
  do so counterclockwise for banishing.

+ Turn the candle over and light the bottom,
  too, likewise to spin the energy.

+ Melt the candle completely for banishing.
  This provides a visual impact of the
  unwanted energies disappearing.

+ If you're going to be doing a lot of Candle
  Magic, seriously consider buying a small
  portable fire extinguisher. Accidents do happen,
  and "safety first" applies to magic too!

+ Divide the candle into sections to represent units
  of time (they should be equidistant but need not

be perfectly clocked). Burn a symbolic number of units that reflect your goal (see Appendix B for numerical correspondences). This is reminiscent of how candle clocks were once made, and I actually advocate using a candle clock to mark quality time with others whom you care about. While the candle burns, they are your primary focus; the candlelight encourages a relaxed atmosphere in which to nourish relationships. This is also a good way to mark weekly meditative time.

+ If you freeze a candle first, lighting it helps *warm* things (a symbol particularly useful in love and relationship spells), and it burns longer.

+ Alter your chosen candle's shape and aroma so that both symbolize the circumstance and need.

+ Shape some wax around a wick into an image of what you hope to achieve using the law of sympathy to guide you. (This is especially useful in banishings where burning the image makes it disappear.) Sympathy simply means "like attracts like," and it is the theory behind poppet-making as well.

+ Use feng shui to help choose a suitable location for your candle. Alternatively, place them in an elemental quarter: Earth for mundane matters like money and grounding, Water for emotional matters, Fire for energy and purification, and Air for communication and creativity.

+ Make your own candles when possible. You can

14

time their creation and design the preparation
process so they can better reflect your goals.

+ Layer the colors in hand-dipped candles so that
each burned layer represents part of the magical
process. For example, if using Prosperity Magic,
make the outside layer brown (for firm foundations)
and the inside layer green. This creates a strong
base from which your money can grow.

+ Knot the wick of your candle, binding
wishes or energy inside the knot so
that it's released when burning.

+ Choose the base of your candle so that
it also represents your goal by its shape,
color, or decorative patterns.

+ Consider working your Candle Magic in a
sacred space (see Page 24, Step Seven).

+ Create a special candle storage box to keep your
tools from getting chipped or bent from the heat. For
further protection, line it with a soft cloth—this can
also be used to polish the wax. If you have separate
boxes for each color, you can add dried herbs or
essential oils beneath the cloth; over time, the candles
will absorb the aroma and energy of the herbs or oils
chosen. Think of an incantation you can use when
blowing out a candle that will keep the magic moving
forward. For example (to ease tension in the home):

While the light is gone, the wish remains.
Let peace fall on this house again.

As you can see, the process of adapting prefabricated spells isn't all that difficult. If you think of the process as analogous to baking a cake, you'll have a firm grasp of the approach. You can't randomly substitute a component in this recipe that doesn't mix well with the whole. You can't add more of a specific energy signature than prescribed without having the entire magical cake fall flat or go completely off-balance in the way it manifests. Basically, just take some time and think it through—and be aware that you might have to try more than once to mix it just right! Practice makes perfect, even in (and perhaps *especially* in) metaphysics.

Creating Your Own Candle Magic Spells

Another big step toward spiritual growth along your magical path is to begin creating your own spells—but plenty of practitioners I meet feel uncertain about that. Their reasons vary. They may not know traditional spell constructs, or they may feel insecure in their own abilities. This section is designed to give either group of people the confidence to take what they learn from the history of spellcraft—in terms of constructs—and apply it to wholly new creations that sing the song of their souls!

Before you say, "I can't do that, I'm not an expert," I'll let you in on a secret: you don't become an expert overnight, and sometimes not even in a lifetime. Someone somewhere had to devise the first love spell, healing spell, crop growth spell, and so forth. Then, more people came along and created spells that made sense in their historical-cultural setting. This ongoing process of invention is truly a legacy on which modern practitioners can draw quite readily—once we accept the role of being our own priest or priestess.

Ah, is that pair of shoes a little too uncomfortable to try on, even more so than making your own spells? Relax. You already assume this role in your life every day when you make moral or ethical choices. In those moments, you are the guru and guide for your life. All you'll be doing now is activating that capacity more fully (which is exactly what an adept strives to do twenty-four hours a day, seven days a week).

As with adapting prefabricated spells, this process is going to take a little serious consideration, but don't be dissuaded! I promise that the time and effort you put forth will result not only in an improved understanding of—and an improved success rate with—your spells but also in all magical methods. This is because magic is akin to a web. Most methods touch upon each other in some manner or another, and the remaining ones actually work together with each other. For example, you often hear the word "meditation" followed by the phrase "and visualization." This is because the two techniques complement each other. The same principle applies to spellcraft! You'll find that the basic schematics you've learned and use repeatedly often help in creating more successful rituals, amulets, potions, and so on.

The Process

In reading numerous books, both modern and ancient, I've discovered about nine readily identifiable steps in the spell creation process. Now, I'm sure you can find people who disagree or who do it differently. That's perfectly natural in a vision-driven faith, but we have to start somewhere. So, look at this list as a rough black-and-white outline to which you'll bring the crayons of your experience and imagination:

Step One: Determine Your Goal
Quite simply, you can't bake the cake without knowing what kind of cake you want! And it doesn't stop there. What about the size, shape, toppings? Using this analogy, it's easy to see

why you're better off thinking about your spell's goal(s) in detail. Perhaps you want to design a love spell. What type of love do you seek? Do you want romance, longevity, just a playful fling? Be specific here, or the universe will interpret things for you. (Trust me.) A great illustration of this came from a person who contrived a companionship spell that included things such as hair color, eye color, and personality. She left out one minor detail, however: species. Her perfect companion (who came to her shortly after the spell and fitted the entire description perfectly) was a dog! In this manner, magic is similar to a computer program—it does exactly what you tell it to do, no more and no less. When you leave out certain instructional language, however, the results get very interesting!

Also consider the potential permutations of your goal. This is where we get into ethics. Is what you want manipulative or harmful? If so, are you ready and willing to accept all the karmic implications of what you're about to do? If not, I'd advise setting the magic aside and opting for old-fashioned, mundane efforts to rectify the situation on your own.

Once you have a detailed overview of your goal and feel secure in your motivations, proceed to Step Two.

Step Two: Choose Components and Symbols to Represent That Goal

Okay, some readers are probably sitting there saying, "Well, this is a Candle Magic book, so beyond the candles, what else can be included in Candle Magic?" The answer to that question: nearly *everything* (everything, that is, that supports the goal in its symbolic value and metaphysical associations). You can play inspiring music while you work, add movement, dab on aromatics, and burn incense. Use any manner of props to illustrate your goal—even time itself (see Appendix B for the special timing of Weekdays, Phases, and Seasons).

I like to make a list of all the items that could be useful for the spell I have in mind, then choose the items that are both available and really meaningful to me from that list. If you try this, please don't limit your brainstorming to items found on various traditional correspondence lists. Rather, include the things that immediately come to mind when you think about your core theme. For example, when constructing a spell to improve your mood or sense of humor, perhaps feathers pop into your mind. (They tickle one's fancy!) When designing a spell for communication, a telephone may similarly inspire you. See, it doesn't matter that neither of these items are necessarily located on any conventional list of components because the symbolic value is completely obvious to you—and you're the one casting the spell! This returns to that notion of being your own priest or priestess. Start trusting those instincts if you haven't already!

Step Three: Make a Blueprint

This step comes somewhat under *the chicken or the egg* discussion. If you don't have a design in mind for your spell, it's hard to choose components, and if you don't know what components you have available (or prefer), it's hard to make a design! Nevertheless, it's generally easier to pattern magic when you have determined the focal points and props. You can start thinking more like a director thinks—the spell a screenplay through which you'll illustrate your wish to the universe.

Taking this metaphor further, every story has a beginning, middle, and end. Throughout the action, everything that happens leads to a distinct point. In this case, the progression of the spell from beginning to end must be designed to build energy and then release it toward your goal. Let's use job hunting as an example. When trying to find work, the first thing you'll need to do is discover the right leads. Perhaps part of your spell would include dabbing rosemary oil onto the want ads so that your conscious mind's awareness is heightened while reading (this is where your props come in). On this foundation, lighting a candle makes perfect sense (shining a light on things).

The next part of the spell might be to take the ads that jumped out at you and recite an incantation over them before you make calls or send resumes—all while the candle continues to burn. If you have seven-day candles that can be kept safely burning until you succeed, even better; interview prospects and callbacks often come within a week's time. Do you see how the progression is logically based on normal human patterns? That's very important. Magic should work *with* Nature, not against it.

The progression should also make logical sense in terms of the goal. When you're trying to lessen or banish something, the items that represent that *something* shouldn't grow during the spell (making a burning candle the ideal medium). Remember that these blueprints you're designing say something specific to your subconscious and superconscious self, the Collective Unconscious, and Spirit. They fashion the way in which your energy manifests. Lay out a couple of potential approaches, and then look at them as a whole, picking the one that seems really right for your mind and spirit.

Step Four: Create Verbal or Written Materials

Drawing on Steps Two and Three, it's easy to see where some type of written or verbalized charm, incantation, or invocation might be appropriate for your goals. If this turns out to be the case, and you want that type of element included, write one! Bear in mind that worded components need not be rhymed, eloquent, or long to be effective. In fact, plenty of old charms were very short ditties that people could easily remember. One that comes to mind is:

Leaf of ash, I do thee pluck
To bring to me a day of luck.

Not a great literary piece, for sure, but it states the goal clearly, and the most common of persons could remember it (rather like a commercial jingle)!

Having said that, there are very specific items to consider in your wording. First, always use terms that you wholly understand and can easily memorize. If you're stumbling over an incantation, it increases the likelihood of losing spiritual focus. Second, rhyme may sound a little hokey, but it helps the mnemonic process for those who have trouble remembering things (especially in a pinch). Third, the meter of a worded component can carry symbolism that supports the goal of the spell. For example, a standard 4/4 beat represents the Earth Element and foundations (the four corners of creation). Therefore, it might be ideal to use this cadence when writing an incantation for a prosperity spell (Earthly matters). Better still, use a drum to sound out the 4/4 beat and your wishes while the candle burns. (The sound of the drum represents Earth's rhythms as they blend with your heartbeat and will!)

Phrases like "for the greatest good" or "for the good call" come up a lot in verbal and written components. These phrases are what I consider "karmic catchalls." While no one would want to accidentally harm another or cause more problems than good, we have a limited amount of perspective in our humanity. By including this type of wording in your spells, you acknowledge the part of the picture (the Web of Life) that you cannot possibly see and ask the Universe to step in with guidance, should it need to. I personally have never felt so adept in my spellcraft or so wise in my spirit as to leave this clause out of my workings!

Perhaps something happens that you can't use a planned verbal component (like privacy restrictions). Quite simply:

think! The mind is where magic begins, and your thoughts are every bit as powerful as your words. Close your eyes, recite your incantation inwardly with as much conviction as you would out loud, and then continue with the spell as planned.

Step Five: Prepare Yourself

You're done with all the fussing in terms of choosing your components and laying out the blueprint for your spell. What's left, other than casting it? Well, you still need to get yourself in the right frame of mind for magic. No matter how advanced the practitioner is, weariness, worries, sickness, and other of life's normal negatives are bound to interfere with magic, usually in a not-so-nice way. Little bits of that energy seep into what you're creating because you enable the process. It amazes me how many people go through the motions of a spell feeling awful and then wonder why they get awful results! It's *like attracting like* on a very intimate level. Approach Candle Magic as you would any other sacred task, and you'll fare well.

Now, let's assume that your mind, body, and spirit are all in the right space for magic. What other types of preparations can you make so that you're wholly focused? My personal preference: a few moments of quiet introspection. If time allows, meditation and prayer also really help direct my concentration to exactly where it needs to be (and where it needs to remain throughout the spell). A meditative, prayerful demeanor seems to open my spirit to both giving and receiving, thereby enhancing the overall flow of energies.

Mind you, this is only what works best for me. You are a unique spiritual being, and therefore, you may have to find a completely different approach. I know people who take baths, anoint themselves, listen to music, dance to sacred songs, or take a long walk (a moving meditation) before spellcraft. Each of these actions becomes a tool that helps us bridge the gap between the temporal and metaphysical, connecting us mentally and spiritually with the process while also improving concentration. My best advice is to try different methods and then do a self-check afterward to see which one leaves you feeling the most balanced and focused. It's well worth your time to find sound magical processes that work for you.

Step Six: Prepare Your Ingredients

Once you're fully prepared for the work ahead, do the same for all the props and ingredients that are going to take part in the spell. Items that have been sitting around your house, being handled by many people, will have collected energy—not all of which is beneficial to your magical process. So, it makes perfect sense to cleanse these items and then charge them for the purpose at hand.

Cleansing can take many forms. You can visualize pure, silver-white light pouring into the item until it feels warm, wipe down the item with cedar or sage incense, or even wash it with spring water. The idea is to eliminate any random patterns that could influence the magic adversely.

Charging, for those of you unfamiliar with it, is a little different. Now that the items in question are spiritually empty, it's time to fill them with the appropriate magic! There are several ways to accomplish this. You can energize the components by sunlight or moonlight for a significant number of minutes (sunlight stresses the masculine conscious processes, while moonlight stresses the feminine and intuitive processes). Another option is to place your hands, palms downward, over the components and think of your purpose, letting energy flow from you into the components (a visualization often helps here).

A third way to charge your candles is by dressing them. In our context, *dressing* means anointing the candle with a symbolic aromatic oil, working from its middle toward both ends. This action also designates the candle's purpose if its color is incorrect (or generic) or if you wish to slightly adjust the color's symbolic value for an alternative symbolism. For example, if you want a friendly love but the only colored candle you have is a bright red (the color of heated passion), you can tone down the energy by using an aromatic more suited to amiable feelings (sweet pea or lemon comes to mind). In this manner, the type of dressing reflects the candle's purpose in your spell. If the candle represents you or another person, the dressing should likewise vibrate with the energies of the individual (perhaps by using personal perfume or cologne rather than oils). Similarly, if the candle is an offering to a deity, represents the day of the week (of the spellcasting), or aims to draw upon an astrological energy, the dressing should be chosen accordingly.

Step Seven: Prepare Your Environment

Before we even begin discussing magical preparations, consider the specifics of your surroundings. Where, exactly, can you put your candles and components so that they're safe and away from curtains, other flammable items, stray hands, or paws and whiskers? Answering a question with another question—do you want or need an altar space on which to set everything up? Having an altar may resolve the safety issues, but a formal altar isn't necessary for this kind of magic. Any flat, stable surface will do. Remember: sacredness is more about attitude than platitudes, and not everyone can keep a formal altar up all the time.

Also consider your overall working conditions. If there's a lot of movement in your spell, you'll want to make sure any windows are closed (so candles don't get blown out) and that the floor is free of clutter. And don't forget to check your own clothing! I can't tell you how many times I've seen very lovely, flowing dresses catch on fire when someone went to light an altar candle adjacent to those already burning. We want the magic to be hot—not the practitioners!

Once you've found a good location where you can work and hopefully not get interrupted in the middle of things—the ultimate focus-killer!—the next question is that of creating sacred space. Because Candle Magic is considered an elementary process (Folk Magic), it is not absolutely necessary to invoke the Quarters (or Watchtowers) for your spellcasting. That said, if you have the time, it certainly won't hurt anything. Sacred space not only protects you from unwanted influences but also holds your energy in place until you're ready to move it outward and direct it. Rather like a plug in a spiritual sink, it keeps stray bits of energy from flowing out before you've completed the desired pattern.

Certain traditions have certain ways of creating a sacred Circle. Many solitaries have their own approaches. For those readers who have neither on which to draw, I'd like to take a moment and share some ideas—should you choose to cast your spell within a Circle.

First, think of sacred space as a sphere of energy that surrounds you in all directions while you work. You can visualize this as a sparkling white bubble or something similar if it helps. To create this sphere of energy, many Witches and Neo-Pagans call on the powers associated with the four corners of creation: Earth, Air, Fire, and Water. The practitioner and Spirit reside in the center of this Circle.

To invoke these energies, face the direction of where each resides and invite them to join your magical moment. Earth is due North, Air is East, Fire is South, and Water is West. You can do this in any respectful manner you choose—just make sure all your components are set out and within the sphere you're creating, ready to go. Here's an example that begins in the East (the place where the sun rises, symbolizing the start of our magic).

Turn to the East and say:

> *From the East, I call the Air,*
> *Come and with you magic bear.*

Turn to the South and say:

> *From the South, I call the Fire,*
> *Come and move the magic higher.*

Turn to the West and say:

> *From the West, I call the Rain,*
> *Come and nourish my spirit again.*

Turn to the North and say:

> *From the North, I call the Earth,*
> *Come and to the magic give birth.*

As you can see, this isn't overly difficult to remember, nor is it fancy. As you call on each power, focus on the energies involved. If you wish, add a symbolic element to the invocation, like waving a feather in the Air to the East or burning some incense in the South. This honors the Natural powers you're calling on for assistance.

When you've completed the Circle, go to the center and welcome Spirit in whatever words feel right to you. If you're working with a specific god or goddess, this is a good time to mention that being by name and put something on the altar to represent that presence. In Candle Magic, a white or gold candle is ideal for a god, and a silver candle for a goddess (unless they have a color associated with them already).

Step Eight: Build and Release the Magic

At last, it's time to start making magic. Follow the blueprint you created in Step Three, being careful to maintain your focus throughout the spellcasting process. As you follow the spell step-by-step, you should feel the air begin to tingle with energy. Alternatively, some people hear a humming, and others will smell a change in the air. Usually, your senses will give you some indication that you're doing it right.

The defining moment of the spell comes when you release it. You created all this energy for a purpose, but akin to an arrow just sitting nocked in a bow, it won't do much good until you let it fly. Some people indicate this motion physically by pointing or raising their arms. Other people mark a particular development in the spell as a cue (such as a pinned candle burning down to the point where the pin falls out). Whatever you choose, continue your focus and begin guiding the energy as far out as you can to your spiritual event horizon. From that point forward, you must trust in your construct and raise the energies to manifest for the greatest good.

This is also the juncture at which many practitioners release their sacred space. This is done by simply reversing the process discussed earlier and saying farewell to the energies. Here's an example of this wording.

Turn to the North and say:

> *Return to the North, return o' Earth,*
> *And thank you for your protective presence.*

Turn counterclockwise to the West and say:

> *Return to the West, return o' Rain,*
> *And thank you for your protective presence.*

Turn counterclockwise again to the South and say:

> *Return to the South, return o' Fire,*
> *And thank you for your protective presence.*

Turn to the East and say:

> *Return to the East, return o' Air,*
> *And thank you for your protective presence.*

When you've finished this *widdershins* dismissal, it's an excellent time to thank Spirit and blow out the Spirit candle on your altar if one was used. Put away any leftover components (and those that shouldn't be left out, such as a candle that needs to stay burning) for safekeeping until next time.

Step Nine: Engage in Grounding and Ongoing Focus

Magic is hard work, and it often leaves people a little out of sorts. The best way to combat this off-kilter feeling is by grounding. Either sit down close to the earth, put your fingers in some sand or soil, hold a bit of obsidian, eat something crunchy such as carrots (a root vegetable), or have an old-fashioned hamburger! All of these actions can help ground out excess energy and return you to a normal level of awareness. But wait—your work isn't done yet!

Creating and casting a spell is but one part of a much bigger picture. Now, you need to support your magic in word and deed. Follow up on your goals mundanely (this is part of being a co-creator), and periodically reinforce your spell until it manifests. This is not a lack of faith on your part. Each time you add energy into a spell, a sturdier bridge is created between the worlds over which your will can travel more easily. Reinforcement also stresses and clarifies the specifics of your goal even further.

Light up My Life:
Integrating Spirituality and Spirit

> *We say God and the imagination are one....*
> *How high that highest candle lights the dark.*
> —Wallace Stevens, "Final Soliloquy of
> The Interior Paramour"

Third in the trinity for soulful advancement (after personalizing prefabricated spells and creating your own spells) is the ability to focus on our spiritual nature. As mentioned earlier in this book, I believe we are spiritual beings looking for a human experience. That humanness includes an amazing capacity to grow beyond our perceived limitations, including mystical ones. While such a discussion could become quite lofty, it really boils down to walking one's walk versus solely practicing the methodology (going through the motions). It also means connecting with your chosen god and goddess in an intimate way every moment of every day. Candle Magic can become a helpmate in that process.

To understand the candle's role in helping us with these goals, let's first consider its long-lasting symbolism within both Western and Eastern philosophies and religions. By some accounts of the word's origin, *candle* means "to make bright." The early church took this to heart, often using candles not only for ambiance during services but also as a representation of God or Christ's purity. Buddhism likens candlelight to the soulful power within each of us—power that we can tap into in order to move out of spiritual darkness and achieve enlightenment. In this system, by lighting the candle, we light our spirit, intentionally leaving behind the mundane-temporal world in favor of the magical-eternal one.

Now, while all that sounds very nice, you might be unsure of how to actually go about putting these ideas into practice.

One suggestion I have is that of a daily god or goddess candle. I keep at least one such candle on my altar at all times. Each day when I get up, I mindfully light that taper and welcome Spirit into my day. I may not spend more than a moment here saying "hello," but it's an important moment nonetheless. It would be so easy to go through the day routinely and forget about the Divine, but that's not the way spiritual seekers should live. We must be mindful—and in our mindfulness, act. This small daily routine keeps me mindful and provides an action that literally ignites a prayerful, grateful attitude.

If you find morning devotions don't work for you (not everyone is a morning person), how about one at dinner? For most people, this is the one time of day when the rushing stops for a few moments. We sit and gather our thoughts or our family together and enjoy a good meal. That's part of the reason why mealtime prayers became so popular. Lighting a candle at dinner can become your mindful prayer and action. (If you live with others, you may wish to take turns so everyone's involved.)

Another possibility would be to allow for some pre-sleep meditation and reflection. Light a candle (I suggest a safety-conscious, self-enclosed one just in case you fall asleep) and think about your day. Ask yourself if the Divine provided any nudges or guidance, and if so, what those moments meant to you. Be thankful for your blessings, and then blow out the candle so you can sleep with joy and Spirit in your heart.

As you can see, these types of activities aren't overly time-consuming or fancy. The point is that you're making a space for the Divine in your life (not that Divinity ever really left; it's only our focus that's been wanting). Spirit is always here—in us, around us, above us, below us, throughout the universe and dimensions. It's normal to lose sight of that at various junctures in our lives, but when you're seeking adeptness, it's important to recapture that vision and awareness. To start off on the right foot, and if you can, take a moment right now and light a candle in a special location. Think of it as a symbol of your inner light growing into fullness. Let it become the light in the darkness, reaching ever outward to the Goddess and God—the ultimate light of reason, magic, fulfillment, and wholeness, then just *be*.

What to Expect

> *Common sense is the wick of the candle.*
> —Ralph Waldo Emerson

What kind of results can you expect from Candle Magic? Quite honestly, for such a simple method, I've seen some pretty impressive manifestations. Plenty here depends on you. How much focus you give the spell, how much support you provide afterward, how much you trust in your magic—all of these things influence the results. Additionally, if you include a karmic catchall phrase (*and it harm none, for the greatest good,* and so on), you'll know that any delayed results (or total lack thereof) come from a necessity predicated on a part of the *big picture* you didn't see.

I realize this seems like a non-answer, but it's the most honest one. Anyone who tells you that a magical process will absolutely work perfectly (*perfect,* in this case, meaning exactly as you anticipate) 100% of the time is a charlatan. Magic is not—nor has it ever been—a perfect art. There are too many variables to make that kind of statement. Nevertheless, I do believe Candle Magic is a very viable tool for your alchemical kit and that you'll find it very satisfying. With that said, let's move forward together and explore some sample spells to which you can bring your imagination and creativity for personally meaningful and positive results.

PART II

PUTTING MATCH TO WICK

Religion is a candle inside a multicolored lantern.
Everyone looks through a particular color, but the
candle is always there.

—Mohammed Naguib

CHAPTER TWO

SPELLS, CHARMS, RITUALS, AND DIVINATION

If you have knowledge, let others light their candles at it.
—Margaret Fuller

This part of the book provides several examples of Candle Magic for a wide variety of themes. That way, when you need a magical method for love, health, peace, forgiveness, or whatever else, you'll have a construct from which to begin. These constructs are helpmates, not edicts. In fact, each prototype also includes advantageous times to cast the spell and alternative components to allow for greater personalization and flexibility. View the construct like a black-and-white outline, the alternatives as crayons, and have some fun!

Note that these topics and themes are listed alphabetically. If you don't find a theme that quite suits what you had in mind, try a synonym. For example, if *prosperity* wasn't listed, you could try *abundance, money,* or *wealth* (depending, of course, on what area of your life you wish to prosper —a prosperous garden would more likely be listed under *gardening*).

I trust that you will find this a helpful and creative guide to all your Candle Magic efforts.

Abundance

Abundant energy is like a swelling tide to the point of overflowing. With that in mind, this theme represents an opportunity to mingle Fire and Water energies into your spellcraft. Beyond this blend, efforts aimed at abundance are best supported when you:

+ Time your spells to the appropriate moon phases (waxing to full), the season of spring, or dawn.

+ Add aromatics such as sandalwood, ginger, or vanilla.

+ Use green candles (for growth), blue candles (for the *wave*), or gold-yellow candles (solar energy).

+ Include other components and symbols like yellow apples, berries, seeds, and anything that reminds you of profuseness.

Spells
For this first spell, you'll need seven light green candles (the color of new growth). You'll also need something that symbolizes the area of your life to which you wish to bring abundance. Put the symbol in the middle of a sturdy table. Starting on the night of a waxing moon, place one candle adjacent to the emblem and light it. As you set a match to this candle, say:

> *Over seven days, this light shall shine;*
> *Come the eighth, abundance will be mine!*

Leave this to burn for a few minutes while you focus your attention on the symbol, then blow it out to release your prayer.

On the second day, put the second candle clockwise to the right of the first, then light the first and second candles (in clockwise order), repeating the incantation twice. Follow this process in kind on days three through seven.

On Day Eight, the candles will surround the symbol in a circle (representing completion). After lighting the candles, take them to eight places throughout your space (to spread abundance) and let them naturally burn out. The symbol can be buried if it's biodegradable (so the energy is nourished and grows), or it can be kept in a safe place until the spell manifests.

For the next spell, you'll need a gold or yellow candle, a yellow apple, a pinch of ginger, 1/2 teaspoon of vanilla, and a pat of butter. Slice the apple thinly across the width so that you can see the natural pentagram on every slice. Put these slices in a greased oven pan, sprinkling them evenly with the ginger and vanilla and breaking up the pat of butter over top. When you're done, rub a little of the ginger and vanilla on the candle, then light it, saying:

> *By this blessed candle's light,*
> *Abundance in every bite!*
> *This apple I bake for abundance sake.*

Put the candle near the stove (but not so close that it melts). Bake the apple mixture at 300 degrees Fahrenheit for about twenty minutes until it's golden-brown and tender. Cool, and perhaps drizzle with sweet cream (to encourage life's sweetness). Consume expectantly.

Gather together a drip-less candle (your choice of color), some potting soil, a plant dish, a corn kernel (you can get seeds at any gardening shop), and a little water. Wait until the moon is in the waxing-to-full stage. (Alternatively, wait until the moon is in Taurus. Astrological almanacs will contain this information.) Name the kernel after the area of your life that needs improved abundance. Place the seed purposefully in the soil. Add a little water, then secure the candle over top, using the soil as its holder. Light the candle and repeat this incantation three times (to improve the body-mind-spirit connection):

> *The seed of abundance I sow, in rich soil to grow.*
> *By the wick and the flame, abundance I claim!*

Let this candle burn until it's very close to the soil, then remove the candle and tend to the plant with loving care. By the time the kernel sprouts, you should begin to see a turnaround.

Anger

The emotion of anger is one that leaves us out of balance. It can also be detrimental to magical efforts: you risk sending out energy that you didn't intend (or minimally of which you really didn't want the karmic kickback). Therefore, spells for anger are aimed at reestablishing self-control and calming oneself so that anger doesn't become blinding. It's best to:

+ Time these spells for the waning moon (so anger shrinks), winter (for cool clarity), moon in Aries (overcoming barriers), and moon in Gemini (balance or banishing).

+ Add aromatics such as lavender, pennyroyal, and violet (all of which promote peace).

+ Use blue or white candles (the traditional colors for tranquility and harmony).

✦ Include other components and symbols
such as amethyst (promotes self-control),
coral (to quiet anger), water (puts out anger's
fire), lotus (for spiritual equilibrium), or
anything that reminds you of calmness.

Spells

For this first spell, you'll need to make a special ice cube and
have a candle handy (your choice of color). Take a small plastic
container, fill it 2/3 of the way with water, and put it in your
freezer. When it gets to the soft-slush stage, insert your candle
in the middle, then let it finish freezing all the way. This way,
the ice becomes the candle's foundation for the spell.

When the ice is completely hard, take the container out
and place it on a flat surface (your altar is a good choice).
Light the candle, saying:

> *By my will and this spell, this anger shall quell.*
> *The anger I felt, like this ice, it now melts.*

Imagine pouring all your anger into the candle and watch
the ice. When it begins to melt, remove the candle (for safety
reasons) and blow it out. Lay it beside the ice. When the
ice is melted completely, throw both away—and likewise
discard your anger.

For this next spell, you'll need to wait until the moon is
waning. You'll also need two candles: one to represent you
and the other to represent the person or situation that has
incited your anger. (Choose your colors accordingly and carve
an emblem into each candle to signify their designations.)
Put the two candles at opposite ends of a table. On the first
night (at dusk, which marks an ending), light them, saying:

The light glows with reason and wisdom.
Let anger burn away and decrease; let there be peace.

Let the candle burn for ten minutes (the number *ten* stresses rationality). On the second night, move the candles slightly closer together, repeating the incantation and letting them burn again. Don't forget to focus on both yourself and the person or situation toward which the energy is directed. Continue this process until the night of the dark moon, when both candles should be allowed to burn for one hour (the number for cooperation), then extinguished together. Dispose of the candles, as they represent your anger.

This last spell calls for any type of first aid cream (as a key component) along with your candle, an amethyst crystal, and a few drops of aromatic oil (I choose lavender). Mix a few drops of the lavender oil into a small amount (less than 1/2 teaspoon is more than enough) of the cream. Stir counterclockwise, saying:

Anger shall wane,
let there be peace again.

Rub a little of this cream on the candle and the amethyst stone. Light the candle and place both it and the amethyst in a sunny window (so that the light of reason can shine on the situation). *Please* make sure that all curtains are firmly pulled back and that the candle is secure! Let the candle go out naturally, rinse off the crystal, and then carry it with you to encourage balance and harmony.

Authority

> *Go within every day and find the inner strength*
> *so that the world will not blow your candle out.*
> —Katherine Dunham

There have been many times in my life when I wished I had a greater sense of jurisdiction and influence over a situation, and I'm sure I'm not alone. Spells for authority encourage this reliable demeanor. (Note: self-confidence is handled under spells for independence, to banish fear, and so on.) Additionally, other spells in this category can help you better handle authority figures with whom you're having trouble. Take care to:

+ Time these spells for noon (the sun represents authority and leadership) or when the moon is in Leo (to develop new skills and strength).

+ Add aromatics: ginger (increased energy), cinnamon (protection from an adversarial authority figure), rose (improved awareness), lily of the valley (clearheadedness), and sage (wisdom).

+ Use red candles (the traditional color for power) or white ones (to encourage rapport and peace with an authority figure).

+ Include other components and symbols such as tea or thyme (courage), clover (trust), rowan wood (power and insight), and peaches (wisdom).

Spells

This first spell is designed to help you develop an improved sense of your own authority. (Note: this authority must be in an area for which you *deserve* authority; otherwise, you risk abusing your power.) Pick out a candle that will represent you in this spell. Put it in a good holder on a flat surface that's been covered by a piece of waxed paper. Surround the candle base with dry black tea. Light the candle at 11 a.m., saying this incantation three times:

As this wax melts, let my influence be felt.

While that burns, gather up the tea and simmer it in warm water. Strain and bless the tea, saying:

Authority within, let the magic begin!

Drink the tea to internalize the spell, then blow out the candle. You can reuse this for any spell pertaining to authority, strength, or bravery.

This next spell can help you cope with a difficult authority figure. I used it once when I was working as a secretary in an office where the supervisor was unusually critical of everyone. For it, you'll need a white candle and a poppet that has somehow been decorated to represent the person in question. In my case, since the individual is me, a secretary, I might attach a pen or other office implement to the poppet. Now, you'll want to split your time on the candle-burning portion of the spell, dividing it equally between noon and dusk so that you combine the symbolic value of sound reasoning with that of an ending (in this case, to animosity). Place the candle and the poppet near each other. When you light it at noon, say:

Let there be honesty, respect,
and clarity between me and thee.

Let the candle burn halfway down. On the same day, light it at dusk, saying:

Animosity be gone; let us learn to get along.

Let the candle burn the remainder of the way down. Keep a small bit of the wax with you for whenever you run into that individual—this'll keep the magic moving and close at hand!

Balance

Better to light one small candle than to curse the darkness.
—Chinese proverb

The yin-yang symbol is one of the best I know that illustrates ideal balance; it represents light in the darkness, the temporal in the immortal, the magic in the mundane, the feminine in the masculine, and so forth. True balance lies in recognizing these things and in honoring that symmetry somehow. Be that as it may, most of us rarely find complete equality in our lives, let alone any one part at a time! The goal for balance spells, therefore, is to reestablish stability, neutrality, equilibrium, and even-handedness where it's most needed at the time. With that in mind:

+ Time your spells for noon or midnight
  (the in-between hours). Alternatively, New
  Year's or Beltane are good choices (both
  representing the transformation from the old
  year into the new), as is when the moon is in
  Libra (the sign represented by scales).

✦ Add aromatics that elementally balance each other, such as frankincense and myrrh, pineapple and pear, or rosemary and spearmint—all of which are categorized as Fire and Water, respectively. Air aromatics include almond, lavender, and mulberry. Earth aromatics include honeysuckle, patchouli, and vetivert.
(Note: it is possible to balance all four Elements, but the aroma produced isn't always pleasant.)

✦ Use oppositely colored candles (black and white being ideal). Alternatively, purple is considered a color that promotes harmony.

✦ Include other components and symbols like fluorite (which promotes balance), a yin-yang symbol carved into the candle, or a feather as a portable charm (against which souls were balanced in ancient Egyptian mythology).

Spells

Perform this first spell at midnight or noon. If you're dealing with an imbalance in intuitive-emotional matters, midnight is better; if you're dealing with conscious-logical-mundane matters, noon is better. You'll need a black candle, a white candle, a candle that represents the self (you), and a bathroom scale. Put the scale on a flat surface where it can remain undisturbed for three days. Put the candles in secure holders on top of the scale. Make sure they're equally separated and form an upward-pointing triangle (a very stable geometric design).

Begin by carving a symbol into the candle that represents the part of your life to which you wish to bring balance. On the first day, light the black and white candles at noon or midnight, saying:

Symmetry enhance, restore the balance!

Let the candles burn for three hours (to encourage balance in body, mind, and spirit). On the second day, repeat the process but say the incantation twice and move the black and white candles closer toward the one that represents you. On the third day, repeat the process again, but this time, say the incantation three times, then light the candle of the self with the other two (blow these out and set them aside). Spend as much of the next three hours as possible in prayer and meditation, using the remaining candlelight as your focus. Keep a bit of the wax as a portable charm to encourage ongoing balance. (Note: every time you weigh yourself in the future, you can repeat the incantation to keep the magic moving!)

For this next spell, you'll need 2 cups of candle wax (remnants from other candle-burning spells are fine as long as their energies correlate with your goal), 1/4 teaspoon each of frankincense and myrrh powder, a piece of wick, a 2 and 1/2 cup heat-safe container (oiled), and a fluorite crystal (small). Gently melt the wax over a low flame (use a non-aluminum pan if possible). Stir counterclockwise to banish chaos, focusing on your goal while saying:

Turn and change, turn and change,
Magic is to turn and change.

Once the wax is completely melted, sprinkle in the frankincense and myrrh, saying:

As this candle burns, balance returns.

Let the candle wax cool a bit. While it does, place the fluorite crystal in the bottom of the container you've chosen and suspend the wick by tying it to a pencil or knife placed across the top of the container. Slowly pour the wax into the mold (this helps deter air bubbles). Cool completely, then remove the container by dipping the whole thing into hot water briefly. Burn whenever you wish to reestablish equilibrium. Add energy to the candle by repeating the original incantation when you light it.

Banishing

When negative energy, bad luck, or mal-intent circle around, it's time for a good old-fashioned banishing spell. I do issue caution on how you devise yours, however. I know of one person who tried to banish the negativity from their office and ended up inadvertently banishing the people who carried that negativity! This is a good example of why specificity is so important in spellcraft. For banishing spells, you'll want to:

+ Time your spells for the waning or dark moon or for the noon hour (to shine a light on the darkness that surrounds).

+ Add aromatics such as pine, rosemary, and woodruff.

+ Use black or brown candles (to ground out the negativity).

+ Include other components and symbols such as beans (once used to turn away the evil eye), a cross or star (protective), and salt (an all-purpose banishing component).

Spells
Start this first spell by carving—into a black or brown candle—something that symbolizes the area of your life in which the

difficulty exists. Be thoughtful and purposeful as you carve, knowing that your intention is to simply banish the negative energies or influences therein without harm to anyone else. Come the waning or dark moon, light this candle, saying:

Candle burn, burn, burn;
negativity turn, turn, turn;
Good luck return, return, return.

Leave this candle to burn out of its own accord (in a fire-safe container), then dispose of the wax so that you literally put the negativity away from yourself.

For this next spell, you'll need to find a candle that has been *dipped* in black (meaning the inside is white, while the outer layer is black). Leave the top half black, but gently scrape away the bottom half so it reveals the white underneath. On the bottom part of the candle, carve symbols of your hopes and wishes, then dab them with a bit of personal perfume or cologne. Leave the top half blank. Place a straight pin in the center (this marks the turnaround point). Light the candle, saying:

Negativity ends as the magic pin bends.
Negativity destroy; I reclaim joy;
As the candle burns, by and by,
All energies are purified.

Leave the candle in place, and do not return until it has completely burned out.

By the way, a neat visual alternative to this spell is to let the candle burn down to the pin, then turn it over in its stand. This *puts out* the negative energy and allows you to *light* (put into motion) the positive energy, giving more support to the represented hopes and wishes.

Collect one black candle and one candle whose color represents the troublesome area of your life. (If the problem is relationship-related, for example, use red or pink.) Place these two candles adjacent to each other on a flat surface. Light the candles every night for seven nights at dusk (the time of ending and closure), saying:

> *Negativity return from whence you came, My life will n'er be the same! Happiness and success I now reclaim.*

Each night you do this, move the black candle further and further away from the other one (slowly moving it closer to a door in your home). On the morning of the eighth day, take the remnants of the black candle outside and let them melt in the sun, banishing that darkness with light. Dispose of them properly. Keep the other candle wrapped in a white cloth (symbolic of protection). You can reuse it for similar purposes.

Beginnings

If you're about to start a new job, move to a new home, begin a new project, or enter into a partnership and would like to get things off on the right foot, these spells are a great companion to the mundane plans and preparations you're making. You'll want to:

+ Time your spells for dawn, the season of spring, or when the moon is just starting to wax.

+ Add aromatics such as lemon and peach (for longevity), heather and rose (luck), and ginger (success).

✦ Use white candles or ones whose color represents the area of your life in which the genesis is happening (red for a marriage, green for a job, and so on).

✦ Include other components and symbols such as seedlings, a buzzer (to denote the beginning), flower buds, and the like.

Spells

This first spell should take place on the morning when everything is falling into place for your new start. Take a white candle and dress it with a bit of lemon juice or oil. Hold the candle in both hands, visualizing the very best outcomes possible from your endeavor. Pour all that excitement and positive energy into the wax while saying:

> *A bright beginning—let it be, let it be.*
> *A light in the darkness—let me see, let me see!*
> *All that was and shall be…open the windows of insight to me.*

Next, hold the candle in one hand and light it with the other. Let a few drops of wax fall on a piece of paper at least six inches below the flame. Continue focusing on your endeavor. Put the candle in a holder and continue letting it burn for blessings while you look at the pattern made by the wax. You can interpret these patterns similarly to those made by inkblots or tea leaves. Here are some sample interpretive values:

✦ A circular blob is a very good omen for unity and the completion of a cycle.

✦ A squarish blob implies good financial outcomes and solid foundations.

+ A lot of separate drops indicate you may be scattering your energy in too many directions or into mixed options that have presented themselves.

+ A heart shape indicates this is a labor of love or that you will receive help and support from a loved one.

+ A smooth river (or S-shape) indicates a likewise smooth, flowing transition.

For this next spell, you'll need the leftover candle wax from the first spell and a seed or very small seedling. Choose a seed that symbolizes your endeavor. For example, an alfalfa sprout could suit your new monetary investment, whereas a lemon seed might work best for the beginning of a new friendship.

Melt the wax (a couple of tablespoons is more than enough). Let this wax cool so that you can easily wrap it around a seed or seedling. As you mold the wax gently around the seed, think of it like a new baby to whom you're giving as much love and attention as possible. As you add more layers of wax so the seed is fully protected, consider using an incantation such as:

> *Wrapped in safety by magical arts,*
> *Goddess, bless this work of my heart.*
> *Wrapped in love and a waxen ring,*
> *Goddess, grant me a great beginning!*

Take this charm with you when you venture out on your new quest!

Birthdays

You know you're getting old when the candles cost
more than the cake.
—Bob Hope

A friend of mine used to tell me that, on your birthday, you're the most important person in the world. That day is certainly worth a moment's pause for celebration—and a spell or two to help you integrate the last year and bless the coming one. Never forget to blow out the candles on your birthday cake with a wish! In Greece, this tradition began with the followers of Artemis, who made moon-shaped, candle-decorated cakes on the day of her traditional festival. When the candles went out, they released their wishes to the goddess herself. For our purposes, you'll want to:

+ Time your spells for the morning so that
  they set the tone for the entire day.

+ Add aromatics such as hyacinth, lavender, and lily
  of the valley (all of which encourage happiness).

+ Use your favorite color candle, an
  astrologically aligned candle (see Appendix
  B), or birthday candles (of course)!

+ Include other components and symbols
  such as your favorite cake, decorations, party
  horns, upbeat music, or anything else with
  a celebratory and upbeat feeling to it.

Spells

For this first spell, you'll need twelve candles placed in a circle so that they're spaced-out like the face of a clock. Dab each with a bit of your favorite cologne or perfume. Beginning with the candle at the one o'clock position, light the candles clockwise in the Circle, saying:

> *One month of blessings,*
> *One month of health,*
> *One month of joy,*
> *One month of wealth,*
> *One month at home,*
> *One month away,*
> *One month of laughter,*
> *One month to play,*
> *One month of solitude,*
> *One month of peace,*
> *A whole year of magic, may it never cease!*

(Bear in mind that you can change the last word of each wish to better suit your circumstances; I've just found it's easier to remember rhymed incantations.) Leave the candles to burn one minute for every year you've been alive, then keep them for the following year. When the candles finally start getting too small to use, light new tapers and re-melt the old wax to use for something special.

On a side note, you can perform this ritual every year for a child, then give them the candles you've kept when they come of age.

This is an adaptation of the traditional birthday wish. Take the candles you intend to use on your cake and rub some lavender oil on them (for peace and joy) while saying:

> *Flower of blue, flower with a calming hue,*

Bring me joy, bring me peace,
Good health and blessings n'er cease.

Remember to focus on your wish while blowing out all the candles on your cake!

Blessing

Who couldn't use a few more blessings on a regular basis (or minimally, a greater awareness and appreciation of those we already have)? These spells are designed to attract divine good fortune, so if you can call upon a personal god or goddess to assist in these, all the better. To harness a blessing:

+ Time your spells for special occasions (such as your birthday or the birth of a child), when the moon is full, when the moon is in Pisces or Taurus, or at noon (the sun is a traditional symbol of blessings).

+ Add aromatics like elder flowers (actually, most blossoming plants will work).

+ Use warm-colored candles (gold, yellow) or white ones (the color of Spirit).

+ Include other components and symbols such as barley, corn, mint, heather, water, bread, or carnelian (all of which have associations with divine favor).

Spells
This first, very simple spell is specifically meant for magical candles. Lay out your candles on a surface (your altar is a good choice). Now, place your hands, palms down, on top of them. The hand is an ancient conduit for blessing, as seen

in many global spiritual traditions. Visualize a bright light from overhead flowing downward through your arms into the candles. Whisper a prayer to whatever vision of the God or Goddess that you wish, asking for their blessings on these tools. If you wish, you can make your prayers specific to each candle (such as one for peace, one for money, and so on). Continue until you feel the palms of your hands growing slightly warm, then wrap the candles in a soft white cloth (also good for polishing), storing them safely away until needed.

Rituals of self-blessing are very popular among Witches. Because each person strives to be their own guide, priest, or priestess, it's natural to perform such functions for oneself. Additionally, I believe that in order to truly help others, we must first be whole in body, mind, and spirit. This means that regular blessings become a maintenance method with the goal of wholeness and ongoing rapport with Spirit.

For this mini ritual, any candle will do, but white is a good choice. Carve images of the types of blessings you wish to bring into your life along the length of the candle (preferably in the same order—from top to bottom—as you're going to request them from a god or goddess of your choosing). Light the candle and concentrate on the first symbol. As it begins to melt, speak your prayer. For example, if the first symbol was a heart, your prayer might be:

> *God or Goddess (speak name of deity, if applicable),*
> *bless my heart that I might be open to giving*
> *and receiving love.*

Continue this way until all the symbols have melted. Put out the candle and light it the next time you need a few blessings to manifest quickly.

Cleansing (Purification)

Ongoing spiritual housecleaning is very important to magical practitioners. I can't tell you the number of times someone has unwittingly dumped negative or off-center vibes on my proverbial doorstep. While I don't mind sharing space, this is something I can easily do without! Additionally, people living high-stress lives or in crowded areas often suffer from psychic and spiritual clutter similar to what I just described, even without someone having visited. Cleansing and purification spells can help offset the nastiness of what can happen when this clutter is allowed to build up. So:

+ Time your spells for early spring (spring-cleaning), when the moon is in Aries, during the waning moon, or when you're doing your regular housecleaning.

+ Add purgative aromatics such as pine, lemon, clove, frankincense, myrrh, or sandalwood.

+ Use black candles to banish negativity or white to purify. Blue (for reestablishing peace) is also an option.

+ Include other components and symbols such as amber (which traps unwanted energies), onyx (or other black stones), salt (a natural cleanser), and any traditional cleaning tools (such as a broom).

Spells
For this first spell, gather together eight white candles and one black one. Set these into very secure holders, placing them on the floor (be sure it's a surface suitable for sitting and meditation) in the pattern of an eight-pointed star. Keep

the black candle in the middle with you. If you aren't using dripless candles, make sure any floor or carpeting is protected from the resulting wax drippings before you begin.

Light the black candle first and focus your attention wholly on it. Breathe deeply and evenly. Concentrate on releasing any darkness or negativity into that candle (see this as the brackish goo that saturates that candle's blackness). When you feel empty, blow out the black candle and turn it upside down in its holder.

Next, light all the white candles that surround you (move as needed so that they're within a comfortable reach). As you light each one, say:

> *Away all negativity and bane,*
> *Only pure-light-energy remain.*

Now, sit in the center of the circle of light you've created. You are now the candle—the wick of your spirit being reenergized and empowered by the purity around you. Stay as long as you wish in this clean space, letting it sparkle throughout your aura. Carry that freshness with you. (Note: the candles from this activity may be reused for similar ends if enough remain.)

For the next spell, pick out a candle to represent yourself. If possible, decorate the candle in some manner to further personalize it. As you light your candle each night, repeat this incantation three times:

> *(Name) is my name.*
> *Like the burning of the flame, purity I claim,*
> *First in body, next in mind,*
> *With this light, all darkness bind.*
> *Then, in spirit and in soul,*
> *I'm now cleansed, refreshed, and whole.*

I recommend repeating this spell over three progressive nights (from waxing to dark moon) in order to banish bad vibes. You can keep and reuse this candle for any purity, cleansing, or similar spells.

Communication

The ability to speak or write—and be not only heard but *understood*—is the foundation to good relationships, effective business management, and many other things in life. Unfortunately, there are many moments in human discourse when it feels like those involved are speaking two (if not more) different languages and with no translator in sight! Communication spells and rituals can help bridge the gap between what's said and what's actually meant. To achieve this:

+ Time your spells for when the moon is in Aries. Fridays and Wednesdays also support this energy. Additionally, consider the theme of the matter at hand as a clue to good timing for your magic. If you're speaking about love, you might want to cast your spell during the full moon, for example.

+ Add Air-oriented aromatics (the Element of communication) such as almond, bergamot, lavender, and pine.

+ Use yellow candles (attuned to the Air Element and effective expression).

+ Include other components and symbols such as yellow paper and ink, a telephone cord, and stones such as beryl, carnelian, and hematite (all of which improve your ability to be understood clearly).

Spells

Gather together a sheet of yellow paper and a yellow candle. On the paper, write a description of the person with whom (or situation in which) you'd like to communicate more effectively. Fold the paper in half on itself, then in half again, and in half again (three times all told), repeating this incantation each time you fold it:

> *Uncertainty and miscommunication be gone for good.*
> *By this spell, let my words be understood!*

Now, take the candle in hand and tip it so that a few drops of yellow wax affix the edges of the paper (like a letter seal). Add another incantation to this process, such as:

> *Ideas and words no longer wait,*
> *Help me to communicate!*
> *Truth be keen, never bend,*
> *So other people comprehend.*

Carry this paper with you into any situation where you feel your ideas or words might be misunderstood. Note, however, that once the core issues have been resolved, you should burn or bury the paper. This is really a one-shot spell.

This next spell—which uses candied almonds and a yellow candle as components—is particularly helpful for clearing up miscommunications in a relationship. Wait to cast the spell until Friday (which got its name from the Goddess Frigg, who protects marriages). Place the candle and the candies on your altar or another area where you typically work spells. Light the candle, saying:

> *The light of good intention shines,*
> *its energy saturating the sweet*

Treats so that my words might
likewise be sweet and well-received.

Visualize the light of the candle saturating every bit of the almonds. Leave the candle to burn itself out (if it's safe to do so), then store the candies in a portable, airtight container. Enjoy one just before going into a difficult discussion with a loved one.

Conscious Mind

Come hither, and I shall light a candle of
understanding in thine heart, which shall not be put out.
—Apocrypha 2 Esdras, 14:25

Some people might wonder what the logical-rational mind has to do with spirituality and magic. My answer to that question: everything! Our conscious mind helps us know what we need when we need it, and it provides ideas on how to fulfill those needs, both magically and mundanely. Spells that support the conscious mind also help with overall alertness, one's ability to enumerate, and knowledge-oriented skills. To cast for the conscious mind:

+ Time your spells for the noon hour or whenever it's sunny (as the sun stresses the logical-rational self) or for when the moon is in Leo (because of the strong solar nature of this sign).

+ Add aromatics such as rosemary, which is said to improve memory. Lilac and honeysuckle are alternatives that support mental keenness.

✦ Use red, yellow, orange, or gold-colored candles (a nice blend of Air and Fire).

✦ Include other components and symbols such as fluorite, aventurine, sphene, maze patterns, and walnuts, all of which accent cognitive functions.

Spells

For this first spell, you'll need nothing more than a candle (your choice of color) and a toothpick. On a morning when you know you're going to need to be particularly *on* mentally, get up a little early. Sit in the light of the morning sun and carve an emblem symbolizing the area of your life where mental accuracy is most needed or required. Focus wholly on your goal, then place the candle into a holder and light it, saying:

> *Logic's power takes hold—uncertainty bind,*
> *With confidence and alertness,*
> *Empower my conscious mind.*

Repeat this incantation several times, allowing your voice to grow naturally. When you feel yourself completely filled with confidence and warm solar energy, blow out the candle and seize the day!

If you'd like a portable charm that supports the conscious mind, begin by saving the candle from the first spell. You'll also need a three-by-three swatch of yellow fabric, a piece of yarn about six inches long, a fluorite crystal, and some rosemary. Light the candle, repeating the incantation provided above. Visualize the light of the candle saturating the cloth, crystal, and herb. Now place the fluorite crystal in the middle of the cloth, saying:

*This represents the successful application
of my skills and knowledge.*

Sprinkle the rosemary over the stone, saying:

This represents information that stays with me.

Drip some of the candle wax into the bundle, then tie it together like a sachet, saying:

A keen wit and a keen mind, herein I bind.

Carry this with you or keep it where its energies will do the most good (like an office desk drawer). If you ever need speedy help from your conscious self, open the sachet and cast one piece of rosemary to the winds with your wish.

Decisions (Uncertainty)

Every day, we're faced with decisions, ranging from what route we'll take to work to what career path we'll pursue! Very few of those choices boil down to a simple *yes* or *no*. In fact, many of the decisions we face have numerous options to measure. It's not surprising, then, that we sometimes find it difficult to sit back and sort it all out. If you're having trouble with a decision, try a spell, ritual, or perhaps a divination method to help you finalize things. Keep in mind that you'll need to:

+ Time your spells similarly to those for the conscious mind, as decisions rely heavily on the logical-rational self. Alternatives include when the moon is in Sagittarius or Libra, when the moon is full (for really keen instincts), and on Tuesday (for good strategy).

61

+ Add aromatics such as vanilla, rosemary, nutmeg, and apple, all of which encourage alertness and improved observation skills.

+ Use both black and white candles (especially for binary *yes* or *no* type questions).

+ Include other components and symbols such as a coin, hat, straw, or anything else people typically use when making random choices.

Spells

Begin with a piece of white paper, one black candle, and one white candle. Dab both candles with whichever aromatic you prefer. If you're not using the suggested ones, consider finding a scent that mirrors the theme of your choice. For example, if choosing between lovers, try rose. Light the candles side-by-side, saying:

A light in the dark,
Insight abide between the options, Help me decide!

Carefully take both candles in one hand (your dominant hand) and tip them so that they drip on the paper. Keep concentrating on your dilemma for about two minutes.

Return the candles to their holders. If the black one has melted more than the white, then the course of action you preferred is not the best one. You can gain additional insight by scrying the wax drippings using this brief list as a starting point for interpretive values:

✦ Black wax covering the white wax: your ideas
   were sound, but the results will be negative
   if you continue on the current course.

✦ White wax covering the black wax: a rough start
   but a good finish—stick with the present plan.

✦ Lots of intermingled black and white dots:
   a very uncertain future tangled in the web of
   fate—you may want to wait a while before
   making a choice and gather more information.

✦ Dots scattered all over the paper: you're trying
   to do too much, scattering your energy to the
   winds; you need to narrow your focus and the
   choices at hand to something more manageable.

By the way, you can use the resulting piece of paper as part
of a portable decision-making charm too. Just wrap it around
a coin and keep it handy for when you're desperate to make
a decision.

A second method of divination requires two black candles,
two white candles, and a pendulum of some kind. You can
make a pendulum yourself out of a length of string (three
times the length of your hand to your elbow is good). To this
string, tie anything that has a discernable point so that you
can determine the direction of movement. Place the white
candles at the North and South of a circular area on a tabletop.
Place the black candles West and East and light all four.

Next, put the elbow of your dominant hand carefully on
the table, outside the circle created by the candles. Hold
the pendulum string so that it rests a few inches above the
table, in the middle of the candles. Make sure it's still, then
concentrate on *one* of the potential paths ahead of you. If the

pendulum begins to move between the two white candles (up and down), that's an affirmative answer, whereas between the black candles (left to right) is negative. Bear in mind, if you're asking several questions, you can get more than one positive answer through this method, meaning those two options would be the best possible ones to ponder and perhaps the ideal focal point for a fresh divinatory attempt.

Death

Most Neo-Pagans see death not just as an ending but a beginning. Nonetheless, the loss of someone in our lives touches the heart and soul of what it means to be human. Typically, candles participate in what Wiccans call a Summerland ritual (to honor a soul's passing and help it along toward its next existence) or in a memorial ritual that commemorates a deceased spirit's birth or death date as a celebration of how much that person meant to their loved ones. Death-related Candle Magic works best when you:

+ Time your spells for dusk (to symbolize an ending)
  or dawn (to represent renewal). Alternatively,
  use the anniversary date of birth or death.

+ Add aromatics such as cypress, frankincense
  and myrrh (traditional funerary aromatics),
  or a perfume, cologne, or scent preferred
  by the person being commemorated.

+ Use white candles to symbolize
  the eternal soul and Spirit.

+ Include other components and symbols that are
  meaningful to you and the participants in the ritual.

Spells

Set up an altar (or any flat surface) with a candle to represent the individual you're honoring, a picture of them, and other items that remind you of them (if they smoked a pipe, for example, get some pipe tobacco). Ask each person joining you for this mini ritual to bring a white candle and a personal message to share with the group or the spirit of the person who's passed over. You need not create a sacred space for this ritual unless you wish to do so.

When everyone has gathered, put the individual's candle on the altar and light it, saying:

> *(Individual's name), hail and welcome.*
> *We reach out to you with our hearts, our minds, our spirits.*
> *We reach beyond the veil.*
> *Bend down close and listen.*
> *This is your moment.*
> *Let your spirit soar as it hears our words and wishes.*

Next, each person, in turn, lights their candle from the first and speaks whatever is in their heart. Feel free to laugh, cry, and generally support each other. Relax and talk in the light of the candles for as long as you wish.

When it comes time to depart, have everyone join hands. Direct your words once more to the individual's candle:

> *Thank you for joining us*
> *and for hearing our heartfelt words. Know you are*
> *missed, but that we celebrate the liberation of your spirit.*
> *We pray for your speedy return to Oneness and Unity with the*
> *God (or Goddess) and hold you forever in our hearts.*

All say:

Hail and farewell!

Blow out the candles.

When someone is suffering from a terminal illness—and you know their time is short—you can make them a special candle to burn when they feel the need for strength and comfort. For this, I suggest a pale blue candle (the color of peace); every night at dusk, focus into it all of your will and prayers toward a calm and dignified transition. For example, when my friend was ailing, I prayed with my palms facing downward over the candle that she would not see herself as her disease but as the beautiful person she was. Similarly, I chanted for things like painlessness and fulfillment. I then gave that candle to her and her family to light as they needed; it was later used as part of her Summerland ritual.

I'm using this personal example because rituals and other spiritual workings for death, like birth and marriage, are very personal. They need to come from your heart.

Divination

Divination by candles is called *lychnomancy*. In Ireland, people chose the color of the candles they used for such divinations according to the question's topic (like red for love and green for money). To perform lychnomancy:

✦ Time your spells for midnight or for the waxing or full moon. Midnight is called "the Witching Hour" for a reason; waxing and full moons emphasize psychic abilities. Alternatively, you can try New Year's, Beltane, Lammas, and Hallows, all of which are thought to be very good times for divinatory efforts.

✦ Add aromatics such as cinnamon,
clover, honeysuckle, fennel, and nutmeg
(all of which aid psychic insight).

✦ Use yellow candles to represent the Air Element,
or follow the Irish tradition and choose your
color according to the question at hand.

✦ Include other components and symbols such as
marigold petals, beans, amethyst, and silver.

Spells

To divine by candlelight, put the candleholder on a flat surface
and sit nearby (about two feet away). Think of a question that's
been nagging at you and focus on the candle's flame. Allow
everything else in the room to fade from view. Here is a list
of interpretive values for what you may see:

✦ A halo around the flame indicates trouble
of some sort looming on the horizon.

✦ A dimly burning candle is a negative omen. If
you're making any plans, slow down or hold off.

✦ A candle that dances rather vigorously
implies sudden changes.

✦ A brightly burning, steady candle is a very good
omen promising luck.

✦ A sparking candle portends important news
about the question at hand.

✦ A candle that smothers and goes
   out quickly is a very bad sign.

✦ A divided flame shows loyalties
   or interests likewise divided.

✦ A blue flame indicates the presence
   of spirits or guides.

✦ Circles or rings around the flame
   indicate joy and fulfillment.

To achieve their results, some people prefer to put the candle
in front of a mirror and focus on its reflection or to look at the
flame through the facets of a crystal (either a clear-faceted
quartz or a crystal that's been chosen according to the person's
question or use). Should you have floating candles in the house,
you can use these as well. Put them in water, lighting them
clockwise, and observe all the flames as they move and mingle.

   A third alternative is scrying the candle wax rather than
the flame. To do this, use one color of candle (or several) and
think of your question while the candle wax drips into a bowl
of water. Observe the patterns that form on the surface both
while the wax is cooling and afterward when it hardens. You'll
find you can often get several different impressions this way
(akin to looking for pictures in clouds or inkblots).

   If you'd like to use one of your scrying candles as part of
a spell to improve other types of divination efforts (tarot,
runes, and so on), by all means, do so! Carve the image of an
eye into the candle and then dress the candle in a psychically
enhancing aromatic, saying:

> *The light of insight burns, the sight returns.*
> *The truth reveals, nothing conceal.*

Light the candle just before beginning your reading. I highly recommend that you take notes of your divinatory efforts and what comes out of them. They will mark your progress and assist in determining what processes work best for you.

Dreams

What's in a dream? Well, if you asked our ancestors, the answer would have been *quite a lot!* There are believed to be documents dating back to 1350 BCE in Babylon that write of various symbols in our dreamscape. Egyptians had dream oracles. Hittite prayers asked for the gods to reveal themselves in dreams, and they even had a special god who presided over the dream world—Ziqiqu. Hebrews trusted in dreams to indicate the will of YHWH (Yahweh), and many cultures look to dreams and visionary states as a means of speaking to the spirit world.

Some of the world's most notable minds respected the art of dream divination. Socrates rewrote *Aesop's Fables* because he believed that one of his dreams instructed this course of action. Hippocrates (the father of medicine) felt that dreams could reveal the source of an illness or diagnose a previously unknown physical problem. Other dream advocates included Julius Caesar, St. John, Mozart, and Benjamin Franklin. And what of Neo-Pagans? We feel that dreams can be far more than just an elaborate subconscious filing system. Rather, we see them as a way for spirit guides—and even the gods themselves—to speak to us. With this in mind, how can we use Candle Magic to help that communicative process along? Here are some suggestions:

+ Time your spells for any night, but preferably for when the moon is waxing to full. Monday (the moon's day) or the moon in Capricorn (discovering things from one's higher self) work well too.

✦ Add aromatics such as sage, rose, thyme, and rosemary (so you remember the dreams when they come).

✦ Use blue or purple candles (dreamy colors) or yellow candles (which are associated with spiritual missives).

✦ Include other components and symbols that are tied to dreaming, such as agate, amethyst, coral, silver, grapes, wine, beer, and dream catchers.

Spells

Choose a night when you know you have plenty of time for rest. Take a dark blue candle into your sleep space with some incense. Light both the candle and the incense and sit comfortably, focusing on the flame of the candle. Repeat this incantation three times:

> *As I will it, so shall it be.*
> *On the wings of the wind—a dream.*
> *On the flames of truth—a dream.*
> *On the waves of understanding—a dream.*
> *On the soil of fertility—a dream.*
> *Come to me! Reveal to me! So mote it be!*

Look at the candle for a few seconds longer so that you can see its image clearly in your mind's eye, then blow it out. Lie down, visualize the candle, and whisper your incantation to yourself as you drift off to sleep. Upon rising, immediately make note of any visions that came to you (voice-recording the memories also works).

Bear in mind that for those who have trouble remembering their dreams, it may take a little time and effort to be successful. If you find yourself in this category, try taking a relaxing, candlelit bath before bed. Add some lavender, rose, or geranium essence to the water (or all three). If you sprinkle a bit of biodegradable glitter into the bubbles, all the better. Combined, these things create a very dreamy atmosphere. Just please be sure to take yourself into bed when you start feeling sleepy for obvious safety reasons.

This next spell is intended to both bring a significant dream and help you remember it. Begin with a blue candle dabbed with rose and lavender oil. Carve an eye into it (this need not be a great artistic work—just recognizable). Hold an amethyst crystal in your non-dominant hand while you light the candle with your dominant hand. Repeat the following incantation slowly eight times while allowing yourself to relax and get sleepy:

Dreaming right,
Dreaming true,
Keep my visions clear,
When the sun breaks through!

Blow out the candle, put the amethyst under your pillow, and lie down. Whisper the incantation to yourself until you fall asleep. Make notes immediately upon waking of any visions that came to you in the night.

Employment

My candle burns at both ends; it will not last the night.
But ah, my foes, and oh, my friends—It gives a lovely light.
—Edna St. Vincent Millay,
"Figs from Thistles: First Fig"

For many people (if not most), employment is a part of the happiness equation. Having a sense of purpose, taking pride in a job well done, and supporting oneself or family all evoke a sense of mundane actualization. So, it's not surprising to discover unemployed, under-employed, or unappreciated employees suffering from depression and other stress-related disorders. The purpose of employment spells, meditations, and rituals is to either improve the situation you're in or create new (and more fulfilling) opportunities. You'll want to:

+ Time your spells for the waxing to full moon (inviting manifestation), when the moon is in Virgo, or anytime in late spring or early summer when the earth thrives with bounty.

+ Add aromatics such as ginger, clove, almond, and orange—all of which support prosperity and security.

+ Use green or gold candles to signify money or other colors that correlate directly to your trade (for example, a botanist might use dark green or brown to illustrate the Earth Element, whereas a nurse might use shoot-green candles to stress health).

+ Include other components and symbols that represent your efforts and goals regarding the position you want. For example, if you're hoping to move into management, a tie or business clothing might be part of your overall ritual. Business cards are also excellent components, especially after interviews.

Spells

You will need a candle (your choice of color) and either a personal business card or those from supervisors or recent interviews. Supervisors' cards are for when you're working Advancement Magic. Those from recent interviews are for opening the right doors.

Prop the business card up so that it's easily seen in front of the candleholder. Every morning at dawn (the time of hope), starting just after the first signs of a newly waxing moon, light the candle and speak a prayer to your chosen deity. Be very specific in your goals, hopes, and dreams. If time allows, stop for a moment and visualize those details clearly. Continue this practice every day until something changes or the candle wax expires. If manifestation hasn't occurred by then, carry a bit of the remaining drippings (adhered to the business cards) as a portable charm that keeps the energy moving forward. For this next spell, you'll need a small symbol of your trade.

A secretary might use a pen, a carpenter a screw, and so forth. Light a green candle and have the emblem at hand. You'll want to add an incantation—repeated four times, the number of Earth and career-oriented energy—that illustrates your goal. For example, if you're up for a raise or promotion, you might say:

> *My talents and dedication like this candle shine!*
> *That raise or promotion will soon be mine!*

Or, if you're trying to land a new job:

> *Have no worries, there's naught to fear.*
> *I'll soon begin a new career.*

73

After repeating the incantation, dab a bit of the candle wax onto your symbol and carry it with you until your goal manifests. Afterward, keep it in a safe place to likewise protect your new position.

Energy (Power)

When people joke with me about broom-wielding Witches, I often say that I prefer a vacuum cleaner. Why? "More power!" As coined by the ever-popular television series *Home Improvement.* In all seriousness, having steady physical, emotional, and spiritual energy isn't only important for comedic moments and magic but also for your health. With so many folk multitasking and wearing many hats, however, there are many times when we do, indeed, need *more power!* That's exactly where these spells come in:

+ Time your spells for when the sun is bright in the sky (Fire), when the moon is full (for the fullness of Water-oriented energies), Thursdays (Thor's day), and throughout the seasons of spring and summer.

+ Add zealous aromatics such as cinnamon, ginger, carnation, rosemary, and vanilla.

+ Use red candles (the color of life's blood) or orange-colored candles.

+ Include other components and symbols that represent some sort of increase (such as an upward-pointing candle, a *greater than* mathematical sign, or the rising tide of a lake or ocean).

Spells

When possible, I like to perform this spell when the tide is coming in on a beach. If your circumstances don't allow for this setting, you can use a slowly rising tub or sink of water as an alternative. Carve a symbol on your chosen candle that represents the area of your life requiring more energy or power. Place that candle in the sand near the water's edge, but not so close that it will get washed out to sea. If you're using a tub or sink, put it in a self-contained candleholder in the middle of the slowly rising water.

Now light the candle and sit nearby, focusing on its flame. Use this simple incantation:

Energy, arise in me!

Start out whispering, then let your voice slowly grow louder and louder as the water rises. When you feel the same swell within yourself, stand up and open your arms to the sky to receive the energy. If you've gone to the beach, blow out the candle and carefully reclaim it. At home, you can allow the water to douse the candle, but do take care that no wax goes down the drain (or you'll end up using all that newly claimed energy to fix the pipes). In either situation, the candle can be used in another similar spell or brought to the altar of a ritual to which you'd like to add some extra power.

For this next spell, you'll need a candle and a three-foot length of rope, yarn, or heavy cord. Wait until noon, preferably on a sunny day, and take both outside to a table. Put the candle in the middle of the table with the rope around its base so that you can reach both ends easily. Light the candle, saying:

As the sun rises high in the sky,
As the flame on this candle grows
full in this magic hour, so too power!

Next, grasp the two ends of the rope (one in each hand). You're going to knot this rope three times, saying:

> *Power within and bound,*
> *Release when called upon and unwound!*

Leave the candle in the sunlight until it burns itself out or the wax begins to melt from the heat. Dab a bit of melted wax on each knot. Keep this someplace safe, undoing one knot whenever a need arises. Never, however, unbind the last knot (this is an old custom). Once you've used two, you should rework the spell and replace the knots.

Enact this last spell on Summer Solstice. Come the first rays of dawn, light a golden-colored candle, saying:

> *Welcome the sun!*
> *As your light shines fully on this day,*
> *So too does energy shine throughout my body, mind, and spirit.*

Next, using the flame of the candle, light a stick of ginger incense, saying:

> *I share the candle's flame with this incense*
> *so it may share its energy with me.*

Sit in the light of the sun, absorbing its power and breathing deeply until you feel fully recharged.

Fear

Among the many emotions common to humans, fear is one of the most debilitating. Anyone who has ever experienced a panic attack can verify how fear (no matter how real or imagined the source) can stop a person cold. In the process of learning to become our own priests or priestesses, we should also aim to be our own counselor for the times when emotion threatens to capsize our life's mental, physical, or spiritual forward-moving boat. One of the solutions I've found most helpful is just doing something positive! The minute we believe we can change our reality, we *can*. So, why not throw a little Candle Magic into the mix as part of that positive action? To cast off fear:

+ Time your spells for the waning to dark moon, when the sun is shining (to banish the shadows), during the month of October (for protection), or when the moon is in Gemini.

+ Add aromatics such as borage or yarrow, both known for their courage-producing qualities.

+ Use black candles (for banishing) or dark blue ones (to encourage tranquility).

+ Include other components and symbols such as amethyst and tea, both of which provide calm focus. Alternatively, eye agate, salt, and turquoise provide protective energies.

Spells

For this first spell, I recommend a black candle—specifically one large enough to burn for about one hour a day over nine days—and one white candle (any size). At dusk each night, for eight nights, focus all your fears and uncertainties into the wax (it sometimes helps to actually hold the candle in your hands while doing this part of the process). Then, light the candle, saying:

Let my confidence burn as surely as the flame.
Let fears melt into the shadows,
banished by light and courage.
Let doubt be conquered by will and resolve.
Strength and surety are all about…I know no fear…
I know no doubt. So mote it be.

The morning after the eighth night, rise at dawn. Pick up the black candle and break it apart (this symbolizes breaking fear's hold over you). Replace it in the candleholder with the white candle. Light it, saying:

It is done, the battle is won;
All fears are tamed; courage, I claim.

Let this candle burn out naturally.

For this next spell, you'll need a small strip of paper, a pen, string or thread, a candle, a toothpick, and some salt. Write the word *fear* on the paper. Next, near the middle of the candle, etch the word *courage* using the toothpick (the word should wrap around the circumference of the candle). Tie the snippet of paper to the candle over the word you've just carved.

Last but not least, light the candle. Direct all your fears and misgivings into that small piece of paper. Watch as the candle of courage literally burns it away. Take the resulting ashes and release them to the Four Winds with thankfulness for your new outlook.

For this last spell, you'll need a tub or shower, lavender-and-pine-blended bath salts, and blue candles (for reestablishing peace). Place the candle in a safe location near the tub and sprinkle a little of the bath salts around it, saying:

Surrounded with courage, safe and secure,
peace rise within, my spirit assure.

Next, get in the tub or shower. (Note: if you're taking a shower, you can use a piece of gauze to hold the salts—just hang them off the showerhead so that they're slowly released onto your body). Visualize all the negativity associated with fear being totally purified and washed down the drain by the salts. Keep some of the salt that you placed around the candle as a portable charm to keep bravery close by (release a pinch of this to a South wind when you need backbone quickly).

Fertility

As with the misunderstandings that surround the word *abundance* in a magical sense, some folk only associate Fertility Magic with getting pregnant. This need not be so. Our ancestors often worked Fertility Magic for their animals and for the earth, and you can too! The reverse also holds true. By working fertility spells a little differently, you can spiritually help avoid conception; this might be good for animals who have not been spayed yet or people for whom some forms of contraception are not healthy. (Note: under *no* circumstances should spiritual efforts become a substitute for mundane protections—in magic and life, common sense goes a long way!) To engage Fertility Magic:

+ Time your spells for dawn, spring, a full moon, a Monday, or when the moon is in Pisces. April is a good month for Fertility Magic.

+ Add aromatics such as musk, vervain, geranium, hawthorn petals, and pine.

+ Use shoot-green or yellow candles.

✦   Include other components and symbols that
    represent your goals. Newly blossoming plants,
    seeds, eggs, and nuts are four choices. Other
    components traditionally associated with
    fertility include coral and agate stones.

Spells

You'll need an egg, some seeds, and a candle of your choice
for this first spell. Choose the seeds so that they represent
the area of your life to which you wish to bring fertility.
If possible, cast the spell on Beltane (May 1) for extra energy.
First, poke a pencil-sized hole in the side of the egg so you can
drain its contents completely. Next, gently break away a little
more of the shell (so that there's an opening large enough for
the seeds to easily pass through). Rinse with cool water and
let the egg dry inside before enacting the spell.

Light your candle and take a deep cleansing breath, in
through your nose and out through your mouth. Imagine
the area of your life in question becoming as fertile as you
need it to be (need drives magic—*desire* is good, but *need* is
less greedy). Take your time here. Let the imagery play itself
out completely. (The more complete the image, the better the
chances of specific manifestation.) Finally, take the seeds and
slowly begin filling the eggshell, saying:

> *The light of hope shines.*
> *What I wish for can be mine.*
> *This seed I plant shall root and grow.*
> *As within so without; as above, so below!*

Finally, take the seeded shell, put it in rich soil, and tend
it regularly. Let the candle burn out naturally or, if possible,
put it in the soil above the egg. By the time the seeds sprout,
you should notice similar changes in your reality.

This next spell is specifically for a couple wishing to conceive a child. If possible, wait until the moon is full (but if that's not when you or your partner's cycle is fertile, obviously adjust accordingly). Begin by decorating the sleeping chamber with romantic candles—including a white one to represent the spirit of the unborn child. Dress in something pleasing to your partner and wear a musky aromatic.

Leave the child's candle unlit on a table near the bed. Adjacent to that candle, lay down a piece of yellow (creation's color) string or yarn. Sit down and join hands with your partner. Light the candle and speak into the flame all the hopes and wishes you have for the future (specifically why you want to be parents). If it is possible to leave this candle lit safely throughout the lovemaking process, I strongly recommend it—the light represents life! Keep the string near your heart. Remember to follow up with your physician in about a month.

Finding (Discovery)

These spells are rather like the Sherlock Holmes of the spiritual world. If you've misplaced your car keys, lost a special piece of jewelry, forgotten who borrowed your favorite book, or been pondering some other elusive bit of information, this is a great place to start. You'll want to:

+ Time your spells for when the first signs of a new moon begin to appear in the sky. Alternatively, wait until the moon is in Libra to restore the balance.

+ Add aromatics such as apple, allspice, lilac, and sandalwood, which improve both conscious and subconscious awareness and insights.

✦ Use a candle whose color represents the lost item somehow. For example, if you lost your wallet and it was brown, use a brown candle (or a green one to symbolize the money within).

✦ Include other components and symbols such as knots (to hold onto things that might be lost), the letter "X" (marks the spot), the number four (Earth-oriented), a dousing rod, a pendulum, magnets (to attract), and boomerang-shaped items.

Spells

This first spell helps when you've dropped an item and have a vague idea of what area it may be in (like between two houses or in a park). It requires a candle (any color, but white for clarity might be a good choice) and a pendulum. Also, if you can gather some dirt from the area in which you lost the item, even better. Light the candle, saying:

> *Light my way. Guide my steps.*
> *Let what was lost be found,*
> *Above, below, or on the ground.*

Carefully pick up the candle and allow a little of the wax to drip into the dirt, then put another small dab on the chain or point of the pendulum. Use only a very small amount; any more can skew the pendulum by its weight alone, so be mindful!

Next, go to the area in which you lost the item. Start in the middle and work outward in clockwise circles, stopping at every hour point. Each time you stop, steady the pendulum and mentally or orally repeat the original incantation. Watch the pendulum's movements. If it seems to move up and down, keep moving forward on the line you're on rather than the circles. If it moves in a circle, check the ground where you stand. If that yields no results, continue on the circular path.

Sometimes, the pendulum will appear to have a stronger motion in one direction (the upswing or downswing). If this happens, follow in that direction. Remember to keep an image of the lost item in your mind's eye the whole time you work.

This next spell is a simple revision of an old folk spell. You'll need three pieces of yarn (one white, one yellow, and one that represents the lost item), each about four inches long, a picture of the lost item, and a candle. Light the candle and begin to braid these strands together, focusing all your attention on the lost item. Say:

Three by three, return to me!

Continue to whisper this incantation throughout the braiding process. Next, take the image of the item and wrap the string around it so that it's securely tied within. Put this on the table just beyond the candle, holding the other end of the braided string in your hand. Slowly pull the image closer to you, continuing to repeat the same incantation all the while. When the picture reaches your hands, wrap all the braided yarn around it and secure it with a bit of melted wax. Keep this in a safe place until the item manifests or a replacement comes your way.

Focus

The ability to maintain your attention for extended periods of time is not just a skill for metaphysicians. It's also a skill that helps students, teachers, professionals, and athletes alike (just to name a few). Magically speaking, an inability to focus means all the energy built by a spell, charm, or ritual can simply dissipate or go awry. No one wants that! So, when you feel like your intentions to stay on track keep getting derailed, try these candlelight spells (then work the more intense magic afterward)! To harness focus:

✦ Time your spells according to the area of your life that demands more focus. For example, a full moon supports efforts for improved religious or spiritual attention.

✦ Add aromatics such as coffee (known for its ability to wake us up).

✦ Use any color of candle, though white might be best for all-purpose attentiveness. Alternatively, yellow is the color of the conscious mind.

✦ Include other components and symbols such as a magnifying glass or crosshairs (both of which draw our attention to a specific point), a bell (its sound has strong centering qualities), and a ring (to frame the item toward which you're focusing).

Spells

For this first spell, draw an emblem—symbolizing the area of your life that needs focus—on a small piece of paper. Then, grab an inexpensive three-by-five frame and a candle of your choice. (If you wish, dab the candle with some perked coffee before you begin.) Light the candle and put your hands, palms down, over the piece of paper. Remember that in magic, a symbol is just as potent as what it represents. Add an incantation like:

Hocus-Pocus, I need focus.

While this sounds amusing, it's very easy to remember (and that's important—you'll see why in a minute).

Next, dab all four corners of the frame with some wax drippings from the candle. Start with the upper-right corner, saying:

> *Air, Fire, Water, Earth—combine.*
> *Let my focus be refined!*

Put the paper into the frame, then pick out a location in your house where you can see it several times a day. Each time you see the frame, repeat the first (or second) invocation to support the magic.

This next spell should be enacted over your morning cup of coffee (or tea, or whatever your *wake me up* beverage may be). Dab a little rosemary oil on your candle to improve your conscious mind for the day. Light it. Then, with a spoon, stir your beverage clockwise, saying:

> *Within this beverage I bind, focus for my conscious mind.*
> *When taken to my lips, The magic is released in every sip.*

Enjoy the beverage at a leisurely pace, letting focus settle in like the warm, centered feeling near your navel. Go out and greet your day!

Forgiveness

As the saying goes, "To err is human, to forgive divine." Humans have not fully realized their divine nature yet; thus, it's sometimes hard for us to forgive. We cling to our memories and pains like badges of honor, even when there's no longer a real purpose for such a display. Forgiveness heals and opens the door for many other positive things. That's where Candle Magic comes in handy. To cast for forgiveness:

+ Time your spells for when the moon is in Libra (for fairness), a new moon, dawn, or spring (for a fresh start), or Friday (the traditional day for relationship work).

+ Add aromatics such as lavender (for peace), mint (to clear the air), lemon (to encourage friendly feelings), and violet (to heal the damage done).

+ Use blue candles for peace or white ones to symbolize a truce.

+ Include other components and symbols such as amethyst (which regulates your personal temperament), white clothing (again to imply a truce), blue tourmaline or sodalite (for peace), ice (for cooling off), or salve (for healing and recovery).

Spells

This mini ritual requires that everyone involved be present (or minimally contribute something personal to the ritual to show their good intention). Each person should bring a candle that represents them to the sacred space. There should be one large white candle on the altar. As you welcome each person into the Circle, ask them to put their candles (in a holder) around the white candle and light it, saying:

I bring the light of truth and a heart of peace.

After lighting their personal candles, they are to put their hands up (as if in surrender) and say:

> *I bring no ill will,*
> *Nor will my words be used as weapons.*
> *I join this Circle of healing freely.*

Once each person has done this, pass a talking stick around the Circle counterclockwise (for banishing). As each person receives it, invite them to say their peace and provide perspective. The talking stick may need to go around several times before things are cleared up. (Do note that while one person is speaking, no one else may speak. Each person is to stay silent until they have the talking stick—this is to avoid confusion.)

Once everything has been settled, everyone should approach the altar and pick up their individual candles. These are then brought to the main white candle while chanting together:

> *Hostility and misunderstandings have ceased;*
> *we promise ourselves to peace!*

This chant should be repeated one time for each person present (but said in unison). Blow out the individual candles. Take some of the wax from the central white one and drip it onto each person's candle; that way, they can take home group unity and keep that candle on their altar.

This second forgiveness spell requires that each participant bring one black and one white candle into the sacred space. Each person should light their black candle in turn, speaking honestly about the issues on their hearts and minds. This is the time to pour any lingering sadness, anger, or other negative feeling into the candle's flame. As one participant speaks, all other participants should remain silent; this is a purging period for the individual, but also a good time to hone your listening skills so that similar situations don't occur in the future.

Continue until each person has had a turn. Then, have everyone in unison blow out and break their black candles into thirds (for forgiveness on all levels of being). These shards get dumped into a trashcan. Lastly, as before, have each person light their personal white candle and talk of their hopes for the future. This part of the ritual is limited to positive insights and goals. Let the candles burn for a while so that everyone can sit and talk in the light of peace. These candles can then be taken home and lit anytime you start getting angry about things that've already been set aside.

Freedom

Freedom is a small word with huge significance. It's very important to the broad-based Neo-Pagan communities, given that their practitioners follow *alternative* ideologies (or religions). Our ability to choose freely is so essential to having a healthy human outlook and approach to life. When you feel that someone or something is limiting these (or other) freedoms that you hold dear, work with these spells. To do so:

+ Time your spells for when the sun is clearly shining (truth and freedom do not hide in shadows).

+ Add aromatics that are very light (nothing overpowering).

+ Use a candle whose color represents the area of your life in which you need freedom. Alternatively, use black to banish constraint.

+ Include other components and symbols that represent liberation, such as a butterfly

or broken knots. (I have a great fondness
for Knot Magic, as you'll soon see!)

Spells

For this first spell, you'll need a 5–6 inch length of sturdy
rope (something weather-resistant) and a candle. You'll also
need twelve small items—small enough that you can bind
them into the rope—to represent the area of your life where
restrictions exist. Light your candle, saying:

> *Let the light of freedom shine in my heart and my life.*
> *Today, I claim liberation from (the restriction).*
> *I will it, I deserve it, it is mine—so mote it be!*

Next, take the twelve items and bind each one into its own
knot with some of the wax drippings, saying:

> *As you have held me, now I hold you.*
> *As each knot is untied, (The restriction)'s*
> *influence over me wanes.*

Take this rope and hang it up outside. Once a day—starting
on the third day of the full moon and ending on the first day
of the dark moon—untie one knot. Typically, this will leave
one knot in the rope (which should remain there to keep the
restrictive energy bound). Keep the rope someplace safe until
complete liberation is achieved. Then, burn or bury both the
rope and the token with the candle.

This next meditation requires only a candle and a good
imagination. Take your candle to a quiet, comfortable place
where you can sit in front of it. Carve the image of a butterfly
close to the top of the candle before you light it. Sit and watch

the candle's flame liberate the butterfly's image from the wax. Breathe deeply, then close your eyes and see that butterfly in your mind's eye. Its image grows larger and larger until it superimposes itself on your aura. If you move your arms, its wings move with you.

Let yourself become that butterfly. Lift yourself above where you're sitting now, above your circumstances. Feel the release; see with a larger perspective. Let the transformational energy of the butterfly's spirit give you the hope and help you need to break free from whatever holds you back. Fly with the butterfly as long as you wish, then open your eyes and focus on the candle once more. Breathe normally and ground yourself, then blow out the candle. Keep it for similar meditations in the future.

Friendship

Acquaintance without patience is like a candle with no light.
—Iranian proverb

The value of good friends should never be underestimated. Our friends stay true even when the world itself seems to be going completely crazy. Thus, these spells are designed to strengthen the friendships you have, heal those where there might be misunderstandings, and invite people into your life who have the potential of taking on that very special role. To harness amiable energies:

+ Time your spells for spring (the season of growth), when the moon is in Aquarius, waxing or full moons, or on a special date that commemorates the beginning of a friendship.

✦ Add aromatics such as sweet pea or lemon, both of which nurture gentle love.

✦ Use candles that are your friend's favorite color. Alternatively, pink is a good choice (the color of platonic attraction).

✦ Include other components and symbols such as pale-colored jade (for comradery) and friendship rings.

Spells

This first mini ritual inspires ongoing ties, warm feelings, communication, and rapport between two or more people. For it, each person will need a pink candle, pictures of their friend(s) or a personal item from them, and a toothpick. Use the toothpick to carve the name(s) of the individual(s) involved in the ritual. Dab the carving with a bit of lemon juice, and perhaps some rose oil (another good love aroma).

Come the next waxing moon, have everyone put their pink candles and pictures together in a special spot. (I like to use a window to symbolize sending light out into the world that will reach my friends.) At the same time of day (one when you know all of you can be home), each person involved will light their own candle. Make sure to focus on the pictures or objects representing your friend(s), as this helps guide the energy. When the match ignites the wick, add an incantation such as:

Far or near, away or here,
I hold (name or names) in my heart as dear.

Repeat this ritual nightly until the moon is full. Then, if possible, get together that night (before the moon begins to wane) so that the magic takes stronger root.

Up next is a fun divination to try with any number of your friends. Gather together whenever you can and have each person bring a spare candle from other divinatory work (it doesn't matter what color, so long as the focus was divination). You'll also need a ten-by-twelve piece of sturdy art paper. (If you have a lot of people coming, increase the size of the paper accordingly. Ten-by-twelve works for three people, four if you scrunch.)

Put the paper on a flat surface and your candles around it (each lit by its owner). Have everyone join hands and think about your friendship—all your hopes and dreams for each other. Wait until you feel the tingle of energy in the air or the temperature rise a bit, then release hands. Each of you will then pick up your candle and tip it over the white paper from where you stand. Carefully walk clockwise around the table, keeping the candle over the paper. When you've gone around three times, stop and let the wax cool.

Afterward, scry the results for patterns or even an entire picture, each person sharing what they see in the imagery. Then, cut the whole thing up into equal segments so that everyone can take a piece home and keep it as a symbol of the ongoing friendship between all those gathered.

Gossip (Halting)

Tired of people who have no lives of their own and therefore talk about everyone else's? Me too! I suspect nearly everyone reading this book has been the victim of gossip at least once and knows how harmful it can be. The purpose behind gossip spells is to encourage the mill to stop. While we can't directly influence free will, we can encourage honesty and an improved awareness of the consequences that arise from such dialogues. That's where this magic begins:

✦ Time your spells for dark moons (the time of least activity—to really weed out the whole issue) or for when the moon is in Libra (to restore balance).

✦ Add aromatics such as pine (for cleansing), fennel (to purify and heal), or rosemary and lilac (for clarity).

✦ Use a white candle for honesty or a black one for banishing. Alternatively, use a yellow candle to represent communication.

✦ Include other components and symbols for truth, some of which are bluebells, eyebright, sunflower, and carnelian.

Spells

For this first spell, gather together the following components: a piece of paper (large enough to write a brief description of the problem), a pen (green ink for healing is one idea), a candle of your choosing, and a clothespin. Put your candle on a tabletop with space enough to write. Light it, saying:

> *I claim the light of truth.*
> *I claim the fires of cleansing.*
> *I claim the warmth of honest friends.*
> *I claim liberty from lies.*

Now, write down the area of your life that's been affected by gossip. Think of all the details as you write, but don't include them all—something simple and symbolic will work best. Drip some of the wax on the four corners of the paper (starting in the upper-right), saying:

> *By the Power of Air,*
> *the winds of rumors shall die down and cease.*
> *By the Power of Fire,*
> *people's minds will see the light of truth.*
> *By the Power of Water, I shall know healing.*
> *By the Power of Earth, there will be renewal.*

Finally, take the paper, the clip, and the candle outside. Put the clip on a clothesline (or something similar) with the paper pinned to it. Ignite the paper and let it burn to ashes (released to the four winds). Let the candle likewise burn itself out so that all the energy dissipates.

This last divination spell can help you uncover the source of a rumor. You'll need a large-diameter candle (the color is your choice, but I suggest a blue one for truth), a large piece of paper (16 by 22 is good), a plastic garbage bag, and a marker or pen. All over the paper, in no particular placement, write down all the potential sources of the rumor based on the information you've gathered thus far. Cut open the plastic bag so that it covers the surface where you're putting the paper, and lay the paper on top (this protects your furniture from hot wax).

Next, light the candle, saying:

> *Secrets in the fire reveal,*
> *while the liquid wax congeals.*
> *Lies are like an open book,*
> *show me…show me where to look.*

Continue to repeat this incantation until there is a good puddle of wax on the surface of the candle (1/8 inch–1/4 inch deep). Hold the candle slightly above the paper while standing or sitting (at an angle where you can see the whole sheet from a central location). Blow gently on the wax so that it spatters on the surface of the paper (this gives life to your magic).

Finally, look to see where the wax landed. You'll often find lines (implying a direction in which to look), blobs right on top of one or two names, and so forth. If there are no specific indicators, look at the pattern as a whole for more insights.

Grounding (Foundations)

There's a lot about magic and spirituality that is based in faith. Thus, keeping one foot firmly planted in reality is a pretty wise idea. Additionally, by doing so, you give yourself strong foundations in which energy can root and grow. These candlelit efforts are geared toward that purpose:

+ Time your spells for the dark moon (traditionally when one weeds the garden or lets the soil rest. Spring is also a good time (planting season), as are times when the moon is in Capricorn, or Thursdays.

+ Add aromatics with a strong Earthy overtone, such as patchouli and vetiver, the latter of which inspires transformation and manifestation.

+ Use brown or black candles (the colors of rich soil).

+ Include other components and symbols such as seeds, dirt, in-ground vegetables (carrots, potatoes), and other symbols of strong foundations with roots. Additionally, stones like obsidian, concrete, and onyx are known for their good grounding qualities.

Spells
When you feel that you just can't seem to keep one foot on the ground—or regain your mundane sense of center—after a difficult ritual, try this spell. You'll need a brown or black candle and some anointing oil that reminds you of the earth (I use a woodland blend). Sit as close to the ground as possible with the candle in front of you and both hands on the floor or ground. Light it and focus all your excessive, flighty energy

into the flame. Let that energy flow. You may find that you actually start to feel heavier. This is a good sign.

Take a drop of the anointing oil you've chosen and carefully dab it near the top of the candle. Then take a little more on your pointer finger and apply it to the bottoms of your feet, saying:

Down, down, onto the ground.
Stay firmly footed, safe and sound!

If possible, keep some of this oil with you and use it as aromatherapy anytime you feel yourself starting to lose that sense of center. To activate the aromatic aspect, just dab it on your pulse points and shoes, repeating the incantation.

For this next spell, you'll need a crystal of your choice, a place to work outside undisturbed on the last night of the dark moon, and a candle. Put the candle into a sturdy holder on the ground. Stand in front of it, holding the crystal in your dominant hand. Direct your eyes to the candle's flame. Think about the area of your life that needs more foundational energy in as much detail as possible. Feel how connected your feet are to the ground at this moment—how steady the candle is on the ground. Earth has always been here. It's not going anywhere, and it's the perfect place to give anything roots.

Take your time meditating in this manner until you feel the crystal growing warm in your hand. Put it up to your heart chakra and say:

The needs, hopes, and dreams
of my heart are grounded in the earth,
Where they will root and grow.

Bend down and put the crystal in the soil right near the candle. Let the candle burn out of its own accord. Leave the crystal in the dirt. As long as it's there, that part of your life will hold firm. (Note: be sure not to leave it where animals are likely to dig, thereby uprooting the energy.)

Happiness

She would rather light a candle than curse the darkness,
and her glow has warmed the world.
—Adlai Stevenson

Health and happiness are two of the key things that we strive for as part of the human experience. When you have joy as a companion, it's much easier to cope with life's chaos and periodic troubles. Nonetheless, there will always be moments when we feel sad or down in the dumps. The causes vary, but these spells will help affect a cure! Be sure to:

✦ Time your spells for any day when the sun
is shining (a symbol of joy and blessings).
Additionally, the season of spring can provide
hopeful, upbeat energy toward this goal.

✦ Add aromatics such as catnip, chrysanthemum,
lotus, orange, mint, or thyme—all of which
can improve our mood. Alternatively, think of
the scents that bring back happy memories.

✦ Use bright blue candles.

✦ Include other components and symbols such as a
feather (for tickle-caused laughter), anything with
bubbles, berries (an abundant joy), and cat's eye
(which is said to bring happiness to the bearer).

Spells

The next time you're feeling sad, gather together a bottle of sparkling apple cider, a bowl of raspberries, and a bright blue candle. Work near a sunny window where there's a surface that you can use for food preparation. Set the berries in the sunlight right next to the unlit blue candle, saying:

> *The light of the sun is that of thousands of candles.*
> *Let it shine in my heart and chase all shadows.*

Open the bottle of sparkling cider, pour a little over the berries, and stir clockwise with your finger, saying:

> *To me, in me, happiness to me!*

Consume with a hopeful heart. (Fun fact: the candle was not lit in this spell because an old country custom dictates that you should not light a hearth when the sun shines on it—Fire spirits are prone to jealousy.)

This next mini ritual takes one week to enact, starting on the waxing moon and lasting through to the full moon. I'd suggest using a spectrum of colored candles in the order of the rainbow; having the blue and violet candles at the end of the line encourages both joy and wisdom. Carve images of the things that will make you the happiest into the candles (one image each). Try and match these happiness goals with each candle's color (such as a heart on the red one, a dollar sign on the green one, and so on).

On the first day of the ritual, light the red candle and say the first verse of the following incantation once. On the second day, light the red and orange candles and repeat the first and second verses twice each. On the third day, light the red, orange, and yellow candles and repeat the first through third verses three times each. Continue this pattern throughout the seven days. The incantation is as follows (with the last two lines being a couplet added during the seventh night):

> *Red brings me energy to weather the storms.*
> *Orange is the harvest of good karma and just rewards.*
> *Yellow is the winds of change, stirring about.*
> *Green is the first sign of spring and hope without a doubt!*
> *Blue is for what I wish most: unbridled happiness.*
> *Indigo is for the wisdom to cherish*
> *those things with which I'm blessed.*
> *Violet is for the spirit within, and without to ignite.*
> *With magic, with joy, beginning tonight!*

Let the candles burn each night for a few minutes while you visualize the manifestation of the goals you etched into them. On the last night, make sure the candles all burn down to the point where they release your mark. You can then blow them out and reuse them later.

Hauntings (Ghosts)

Things that go *bump* in the night can keep life interesting or cause disruptions. Think you may have an unruly ghost on your hands? Here are some magical ideas for finding out 1) if it's really present, 2) why, and 3) how to get rid of that energy if you so choose:

+ Time your spells for the full moon or midnight—or other times when the Spirit World is thought to be active, like Beltane, Lammas, and Samhain.

+ Add aromatics such as sweetgrass, chrysanthemum, heather, and violet (all associated with spirits of the dead).

+ Use a white candle or a candle whose color somehow represents the ghost's personality and demeanor.

+ Include other components and symbols trusted for their ability to call spirits, such as dandelion, thistle, salt, and iron (protective), and azurite or lapis (to improve your psychic sensitivity).

Spells

This activity uses candlelight to confirm the existence of a ghostly presence—and its location inside your house. I suggest using a plain candle without any carvings or aromatics. Wait for a suitable time to work (preferably at night). Begin in the area where you typically sense the spirit. Make sure there are no open windows, drafts, or other potential interruptions.

Put the candle on a flat surface and light it. Watch for the following signs, as they traditionally indicate the presence of a spirit:

+ The wax melts down one side and curves around (this is called a *winding sheet*).

+ The flame of the candle seems brighter on one side than the other (this means the ghost is closer to the brighter spot).

+ The flame gets blown out by a cold breeze (take note of the breeze's direction so that you can narrow down the ghost's general location).

These beliefs are very old and rooted in a long tradition that can support your observations. Write down what you experience, where, and when. Keep this log until a pattern arises, and then use that pattern to gather more information.

This next spell is designed to protect you from ghosts if need be (though to be honest, living with them can be far more interesting). You'll need several votive candles—one for every window in the room where you feel the ghost's presence. Additionally, you'll need to bring a white taper candle and a red ribbon or piece of yarn.

Begin in a Northward window, placing one votive there and lighting it, saying:

> *Home is my sacred space;*
> *Malicious spirit be gone from this place.*

Repeat this process with all the other windows.

Next, stand in the middle of the room while holding the remaining white taper. Tie the red ribbon or yarn near the middle of the taper, repeating the following incantation three times:

> *Around this candle red ribbon wind,*
> *by my will this spirit—bind!*

Keep the candle carefully stored away and only light it during times when you feel the negativity returning. The votives should be allowed to burn out. (They don't drip, so wax won't be an issue. Just make sure there aren't any curtains nearby).

And what if you wish to make contact with spirits? There are times when we want to welcome them among us (such as while commemorating a deceased loved one's birthday). There are other times when we'd just like their insights. In either case, light a candle to represent the spirit you're welcoming (and perhaps dab it with some of the person's favorite cologne or perfume). Place this across from that person's picture on a table.

You'll also need the name of the person written on parchment. This is put midway between the candle and the picture. Now, focus on your desire to spend time with that spirit. Take the pointer finger of your dominant hand and trace a path from the picture to the parchment, saying:

> *I open the door to you and only you.*
> *(Spirit's name), be welcome in my home and sacred space.*

Pick up the parchment in your dominant hand. Finish tracing the path to the candle, then ignite the parchment. Be sure to have a fire-safe container nearby—like a stoneware bowl filled with sand or dirt and placed on a trivet—into which you can put the parchment while it burns. Visualize the face of the person in the flame of the candle and say:

> *As this parchment burns away,*
> *so do the barriers between my world and thine.*
> *I open the door to you and only you. Be welcome.*

From here, what happens usually varies. You may sense a presence, smell a unique aroma, hear something, or even have no experience whatsoever until you go to sleep that night and dream! Keep your eyes open and remain aware of subtle clues that your guest has arrived.

Healing and Health

Typically, I suggest that you have someone else perform healing spells or rituals when you're ailing. No matter how adept we may be, some of the negative energy from sickness can taint our magic. Also, if you do choose to enact a healing spell on someone, make sure you have permission. All the magic in the world won't help someone recover if they don't want to get better! Should it be impossible to get permission, work the spell in such a way that you leave the energy open for acceptance or rejection by the intended recipient. Also ensure that you are managing your helath in all the mundane ways as well—if you are experiencing illness or injury, always follow medical advice in conjunction with magical healing practices! To heal through magic:

+ Time your spells for a waning moon (to banish sickness) or a waxing moon (to encourage recovery). Working in sunlight also improves well-being.

+ Add aromatics such as fennel, mint, apple, or orange, all of which are associated with a sound body, mind, and spirit.

+ Use pale shoot-green candles (the color of new growth) or white ones (for purification).

+ Include other components and symbols that represent health or healing to you. For example, I enjoy making a chicken soup potion in combination with my healing spells. Other options include salves, bandages, a first aid kit, and so on.

Spells

For this spell, I recommend you choose a candle color that represents the ailment in question. Anoint this with lavender and rose oil, which encourages peace and self-love (or love toward the person for whom the spell has been designed). If possible, also have a token to represent the ill person so that you can better direct the energy (a photo is one option, or something they've given you over the years).

Put the candle on a small table around which you can walk easily. Light the candle and hold the item that represents the ill person. Walk counterclockwise around the table eight times, repeating this incantation once on every complete circuit:

To the Earth, to the Earth,
all negativity to Earth.
To Earth, to Earth, all sickness to Earth.
(Name of the ailing person), accept this spell, become well!

(As you can see, there is a clause here that allows the individual to accept or reject the energy, thereby not overstepping free will guidelines.)

Upon completion, either let the candle burn itself out and bury the remains (in the earth where you have commanded the sickness) or wrap the candle in a soft cloth and keep it in a safe place to protect the person until they recover.

For this next spell, you'll need a candle (the color is your choice), a small piece of paper, a pen, a fireproof container, and some cleansing oil (like cedar). Near the top of the piece of paper, write the name of the malady in question. Next, underneath that word, write it again, but leave off the last letter. Continue to rewrite in this way (subtracting another letter each time) until there is only one letter left of the malady; the result will be an inverted triangle of letters.

Light the candle and dab the final point of the triangle with the oil. Focus on cleansing away every last vestige of the malady from whoever is ailing. Set the paper on fire and transfer it to the fireproof container, continuing to focus on your goal until the paper is completely consumed. To complete the process, take the ashes outside and release them to the winds.

Holidays

Throughout the year, several holidays use candles to bring a lovely glow and ambiance to their festivities. While it would be impossible to cover every holiday in a book like this, I would like to share a few ways in which candles have enlivened celebratory settings. Because each holiday is different, I can't suggest broad-based timing, aromatics, and colors for the purpose of spellcasting. Instead, I'm going to list out the dates and descriptions of these celebrations, how candles were and are used in them, and what they symbolize so that you might do similar things on those dates (or use their timing to accent other magical efforts):

+ **January—Carnival:** A pre-Lent European festival that includes large candles as a form of celebration and merrymaking before the more serious season begins.

+ **February 2—Candlemas:** This celebration is of light triumphing over darkness, intended to give the sun strength for its post-winter return to full power.

+ **March 31—Feast of the Moon Goddess:** A festival that comes from Rome. The tradition is to light thirteen candles on this day to honor the moons of the year.

+ **(Early) April—The Boat Festival in France:** On this day, people place small candles in boats along with their wishes!

✦ **April 8—The Buddha's birthday:** Light
eight candles on this day to encourage
enlightenment and serenity in your own life.

✦ **May 3—Bona Dea:** A Roman celebration
of abundance. If you jump over a candle on
this day, you'll receive good fortune.

✦ **June 21—Summer Solstice:** Light any candle
on this day to honor the sun in all its glory.

✦ **August 15—The Birthday of Isis:** Lighting
a candle on this day encourages blessings
for those who travel frequently.

✦ **September 25—Festival of Durga Puja:** This Indian
goddess safeguards our home and those we love, and
she can be invoked on this day using a yellow candle.

✦ **October 31—Halloween:** What would any
Hallows celebration be without a candle in a
pumpkin to protect us from evil spirits?

✦ **November 16—Diwali:** An Indian festival honoring
the goddess of wealth. You can encourage her favor by
lighting yellow- or gold-colored candles on this day.

✦ **December 21—Yule:** A festival of lights (similar
to Candlemas) with a stronger focus on the
hearth and home. Candles are lit to honor the
nature spirits who keep evergreens and other
perennial flora alive through the harsh months.

Humor

Laughter is good soul food—and humor is a great coping mechanism—for life's bumps and bruises. The problem is that our daily routines can quickly rob us of this very important attribute just on wear and tear alone. When you feel your sense of humor waning, keep these things in mind for candlelit activities:

+ Time your spells for whenever you're feeling unamused. I wouldn't wait for things to get worse.

+ Add light aromatics (humor shouldn't have heavy energy) that you personally enjoy (it's hard to be upbeat when you hate what you're smelling).

+ Use a multicolored candle if you can find one. I personally see humor as a rainbow-like glitter that sprinkles into one's aura. Multicolored candles reflect that idea.

+ Include other components and symbols such as feathers, jokes, and puns, as well as bubbles, balloons, and anything else that might inspire your inner child's sense of whimsy.

Spells
Choose a candle that's to your liking and find a feather. You can find the feather outside—however, please put it in a plastic bag in the freezer for one week to kill off any insect hitchhikers. Place the candle on a surface that you can easily see when standing. Light the candle and breathe deeply. Really try to relax and loosen up—it's nearly impossible to find the humor in things when you're tightly wound.

Next, brush the feather over all of your aura (your head, arms, torso, legs, and even below your feet). As you do so, chant this little ditty:

> *Negativity, take flight, tickled by light;*
> *Negativity, flee; good humor restore in me!*

Afterward, let the candle continue to burn (if it's safe to do so) and go do something fun that will really inspire your funny bone (maybe go to a comedy club or rent your favorite rom-com).

Inspiration

> *We owe a lot to Thomas Edison—if it wasn't for him,*
> *we'd be watching television by candlelight.*
> —Milton Berle

What is life without muse—without that wonderful bit of starlight and moonbeam that touches our pens, paints, and carvings with random bursts of inspiration? Nonetheless, many days, I wouldn't know inspiration if it walked up and tapped me on the shoulder! Whenever you feel similarly and want to refill your well of creativity, begin here:

+ Time your spells for when the moon is in Cancer, the waxing moon, the month of April (and all of spring), or days when the wind is blowing gently (so that ideas can take flight).

+ Add aromatics such as allspice and lotus, both known to manifest the muse.

✦ Use yellow or silver candles (or another
color you associate with creativity).

✦ Include other components and symbols
such as a lamp (ideas), stars (wishes),
and quartz (for productivity).

Spells

To encourage inspiration for a project or art form, bring the
main tools of that project or art form to your altar—or another
special spot where they can remain undisturbed. Do this on
the first night of the full moon, placing the items in the light
of three candles (one for each night of the full moon). On the
first night, light the first candle and say:

> *Tonight, the moon is full;*
> *So, too, fill my mind and spirit with ideas.*
> *As this candle burns bright,*
> *Ignite the spark of inspiration within.*

Blow out the candle and sit, meditating in the moonlight
for a while, undisturbed.

On the second night, light the first candle, repeating
the first incantation. Then light the second candle from
the first, saying:

> *As one flame to the other,*
> *So, too, does the light of inspiration spread to my soul.*

Blow out that candle and spend more time in quiet
meditation. (You may wish to keep a notebook with you
while you meditate on these two nights; a lot of people say
they get ideas during this time.)

On the last night, light the first and second candles, recreating their invocations as before. Then light the third on the second, saying:

> *As I will it, so mote it be.*
> *The flame of inspiration,*
> *I claim—it burns within me!*

Leave the candles burning and do some work with the items you've left on the surface, which by now have absorbed your magic.

This next spell is for general inspiration. To begin, you'll need a candle and a feather. You will also need to enact it in a place where you can release the feather to a live water source (*live* meaning moving). Sit down near the water and light your candle. Hold the feather, cupping it in both hands. Bring the feather to your heart chakra and visualize the area of your life in which you desire greater inspiration. Put that desire in the form of a wish and state it out loud. For example, if I wanted more inspiration in my writing, I would say:

> *This feather is as the quill of my pen.*
> *As it's touched by the fire, so too touch my heart.*
> *As it's released to living waters,*
> *Let the waves of inspiration flow to me and through me.*

For inspiration in creating a business plan, I might say:

> *This feather is the lifting wing of my work.*
> *As it's touched by the fire, so too give light to my plans.*
> *As it's released to the vibrant waves,*
> *So, too, let the waters of creativity fill my work.*

Continue holding the feather close until you feel it completely saturated with your will. Put the tip into the fire until it sparks, then release it immediately to the water. The flow can take your wishes to the world. Blow out the candle and keep it for other creativity-oriented spells.

When you need to overcome some type of blockage (typically discouragement or self-doubt) in order to feel inspired again, this last spell is a good one to enact. For it, you will need one candle to represent you, one black candle to represent the blockage, and one candle to represent the area of your life in which you're feeling halted. Carve each candle with symbols suited to its function. For example, if the blockage is in matters of love, carve a heart on the third candle (perhaps a red one). Carve your initials into your candle.

Place the three candles in a line on the table with the black candle in the middle. This candle will not be lit (you don't want to give the blockage more power). Rather, light your candle first, saying:

Even as dawn breaks the night and becomes day,
No more does this problem stand in my way!

Keep repeating this incantation until you feel your confidence growing naturally. Reach out with your dominant hand and remove the black candle from between the other two, then break it. Put it aside. Finally, light the last candle, saying:

My will and my resolve are sure.
From the flame of my heart,
I light a new fire under (area of life)
and reclaim inspiration.

Fill in the blank with the area of your life where inspiration has been lacking. If possible, let these candles burn out of their own accord.

Jealousy

Jealousy is one of the most destructive and unproductive emotions in humankind. It can completely tear apart long-term relationships, cause dissension among friends and families, and eat away at a person's spirit like a cancer. There is a large difference between caring about someone and thinking of them as a personal possession. Similarly, even when there may be a good reason for you to feel a little envious or mistrustful, it is always good to take a few steps back and try to gain more perspective. This use of Candle Magic can give you a few ways to readjust your outlook and bring positive energy to bear. So:

+ Time your spells for the waning or dark moon, dusk, or when the moon is in Aries (cleaning out old habits) or Libra (restoring balance).

+ Add aromatics such as mint and violet that both clear the air and restore peace.

+ Use green candles to represent jealousy or white ones for purifying intention.

+ Include other components and symbols that represent the individual toward whom the jealousy arises—or carnelian, which improves communication skills and stills jealousy.

Spells
This first spell is designed to halt unwarranted jealousy aimed at you. To enact it, you must be certain of the source of the problem. Gather together a white candle, a piece of paper, a pen, an ice cube tray, and water. If possible, wait until the waning moon (to shrink the negative energy). Write the source of jealousy on the paper (perhaps in green ink). Light the candle, saying:

No need for possessiveness; no need for ill will.
By this spell, your jealousy chill!

Fold the paper in half, then in half again, and in half again (three times all told), then seal it with candle wax. Put it in the ice cube tray with water and freeze it. Leave it in the back of the freezer for as long as it takes to cool down the problem.

(Keep in mind: you can enact this spell on *yourself* if you're the one having overly possessive tendencies and harboring ill will because of them.)

This next spell requires a greenish-yellow candle, a cup of water, and a carnelian stone. Put the stone in the cup of water and set it aside. Light the candle and focus all your jealousy into it. Think of all the situations that make you feel jealous. Consider exactly how you feel in those moments. Let all that energy pour into the candle's flame. Now, carefully pick up the candle in your dominant hand and look at it, saying:

Jealousy has no power over me.
It's control I quell
By my will and this spell!

Turn the candle upside down and douse it in the water. Throw away the candle to disengage yourself from the jealousy. Keep the water-bathed stone as a talisman. Anytime you feel the green-eyed monster creeping back, hold the stone in your hand and repeat the incantation to yourself.

Justice (Legal Matters)

Are you facing a problem with lawyers? Do you have to sign a complex contract? Do you feel as if people or circumstances have trampled any sense of equity, truth, and fairness? I know I've faced each one of these situations and, in them, felt as if I had no voice or power. There are times when red tape binds you mundanely—but magically, it holds no strength. Spells of this nature can serve as scissors, cutting through any issues you may be facing in the legal arena. To apply Candle Magic in this way:

+ Time your spells for when the moon is in Libra, Tuesdays, or when the sun is shining brightly.

+ Add aromatics such as ash wood (as an incense base) and vanilla.

+ Use a white or gold candle.

+ Include other components and symbols such as carnelian, the Justice card of a tarot deck, hematite, a gavel, scales, and amethyst (for tempering energies).

Spells
Gather together a gold candle, some finely ground wood, and a vanilla bean finely shaved. Put the candle in the center of a bowl filled with dirt or sand, then sprinkle the wood and vanilla around it. Each day, rub a little of the wood and bean into the candle and light it. Take a moment and think about the problem that requires justice. Visualize it resolved in the best, most positive way. Leave the candle to burn while you

prepare for your day, then blow it out before leaving. Continue this mini ritual every day until the problem ceases.

(If you have to replace the candle during this time, light the new candle from the flame of the first, then put the bottom of the new one into some of the melted wax from the previous. This *builds* the energy by making an unbroken line of wax.)

This next bit of magic requires a tiny candle (like those for a birthday cake), a pouch, and a carnelian. During the noon hour, go outside with the candle and the carnelian and bless them, saying:

> *Spirit, shine the light of truth and fairness upon me.*
> *When I ignite this candle,*
> *Let all around see clearly through the darkness.*
> *When I touch this stone,*
> *Let my words be clear and understood*
> *so that there will be a fair resolution.*

Put the candle and stone into the pouch and keep it with you during your legal obligations until a suitable moment arrives. Excuse yourself and go to the lavatory to light the candle briefly. Repeat your prayer mentally, directing your energy toward this specific situation (add more information if you feel it prudent). Then, take out the stone and put it in your pocket. Blow out the candle (put a little water on the tip before replacing it in the pouch so it won't burn the fabric). Finally, return to the task at hand, rubbing the stone periodically to release the necessary energy.

Kindness, Charity, and Service

There are days when I wonder if kindness and common courtesy have gone by the wayside. There are other times when I wish that I (or someone else) had a better awareness of a certain need for charity or service. Let's face it—we've been part of a "me first!" generation for *more* than a generation! Our lives have become so hectic that the little niceties often get overlooked. This is a shame, but it's a situation to which a little well-applied magic might provide some remedies. These aren't quick fixes; one must be mindful to remember that true change begins within. Instead, this application of Candle Magic should be a helpmate to the process of remembering these important considerations. To use it:

✦ Time your spells for when it's warm outside (physical warmth symbolizes the emotional warmth you're trying to achieve). Monday is also a good day because the moon is associated with feelings.

✦ Add aromatics such as elderflower or rose, but keep the fragrance light—kindness should not overwhelm!

✦ Use white or orange candles. White represents pure intentions, while orange is the harvest —the return of good karma.

✦ Include other components and symbols that represent benevolence and thoughtfulness to you (flowers seem to be a popular option).

Spells

This first spell requires a large bowl into which you can place a taper candle securely. Also, pick out a bill (any denomination) that can act as *seed money* and put it in the bowl. Light the candle every day when you come in the door from an outing and toss your spare change into the bowl. If you have an area of your life that needs a little more charity, kindness, or service, think of it during this process. Blow out the candle when you're done focusing on those goals. Continue this process every day until the bowl is full.

Now, this is the important part. When the bowl is full, you *must* give that money (all *but* the seed bill) to someone in need or a charity of your choice. The idea here is to invoke charity and service by doing the same yourself. If the candle grows low at any time, light a new one from the flame of the first and replace it. Keep the remnant wax to remelt for any magic that has a giving focus.

Those who serve, likewise, need service. The tragic reality of our community is that many of our elders and teachers are burning out. Use this next candlelight spell to give such folk a little more energy—and to honor their contributions.

To begin, pick out a handful of teachers who have touched your life deeply. Choose a candle to represent them, carving their initials into the wax. Put the candles into holders and then place them somewhere special (an altar is ideal). Every month, on the night of the full moon, light the candles and direct the moon's energy toward the flame and the person's spirit it represents. Leave the candles burning for three hours to charge body, mind, and spirit equally. Do this for an entire year, replacing the candles as necessary, and then perhaps send those people a little letter, sharing your intentions along with a little leftover wax that they can use as an amulet or charm.

Kinship

The word *kinship* can be known to mean "of the same nature or mind." True kinship has very little to do with blood ties and more to do with how we feel toward special people in our lives. I know that I have friends who are truly *kin* in heart and spirit. We share certain bonds that were built with tenacity and time. While one cannot avoid the ongoing maintenance it takes to keep kinship alive between two or more people, you can enact candlelight spells, meditations, and rituals to support your ties to one another. This support is not meant to constrain but rather to keep the spiritual lines of communication open and vital. To cast for kinship:

+ Time your spells for when the sun is shining (it implies blessings), during a waxing moon, or during the months of June and July (most popular for reunions and weddings).

+ Add aromatics such as rosemary (remembrance), lemon (friendship), orchid (love), and nutmeg (fidelity).

+ Use pink candles for gentle love.

+ Include other components and symbols such as trees (a family tree in particular), coats of arms, knots, rings, and jade (a stone that inspires good feelings between people).

Spells

Enact this mini ritual on special occasions—such as holidays, anniversaries, and birthdays—where the members of your group or family can't get together to celebrate. You'll need to do a little prep work to pull it off, though! First, send a special candle to every person who wants to participate. These should all match in color, aroma, and so on—and bear a mark that somehow represents the whole group.

Next, you need to choose a date and time when you can all work (remember to account for time differences). On the appointed day and hour, go to a window and set up your candle. Look toward the horizon and think of your friends or family who are also doing the same. Light the candle and softly chant:

Though we are apart, we are of one heart.
Our spirits and minds, this magic binds.
Across the land, our love we send.
By this candle's light, our souls unite!

Continue repeating the chant for about fifteen minutes (or whatever time you've agreed upon). When you stop, close your eyes and let hugs from near and far surround you astrally. Accept the warmth extended by others and rejoice in it.

During this next activity, you'll be making a special candle for someone who is going away (be it to college, a new home, or some other long-term destination). You'll need some pink candle wax and two jade stones (small pieces are best). You'll also need some type of candle mold (inexpensively and easily bought at most hobby and craft shops).

Wait until the second night of the full moon to prepare this candle. Melt the wax over a low flame, and if you wish, add some aromatics that will remind that person of you or of home. Pour a little of the melted wax into the bottom of the mold and let it cool slightly. Place the two stones together (touching each other) into that wax, saying:

My heart to your heart—never apart.
When you feel lonely, know you're near to me.
Then, when this candle burns, my love will return!

Pour in the remaining wax, place the wick, and let cool. When you unmold the candle, wrap it in a soft cloth with a copy of the above incantation so that the recipient understands how to use it.

This last mini ritual strengthens the sense of kinship in a group. For it, each person must bring a candle to the gathering marked in a manner that's easily recognizable. Additionally, the person coordinating the event should bring some white, yellow, and blue ribbons (the colors of peaceful communication and joy) braided together. The altar should be empty but for each person's candle. In turn, around the Circle, everyone should light their candle and state their feelings toward the whole (also any wishes and goals). When everyone is done, the coordinator (often the priest or priestess) may blow out the candles and bind them with the ribbon. These should be stored safely away to protect the group's unity. If someone leaves the group in the future, the bundle can be opened, and the individual's candle retrieved out of it, then resecured.

Learning (Knowledge and Understanding)

> *Curiosity is the wick in the candle of learning.*
> —William Arthur Ward

Linguistically, *knowledge* is a wonderful word. It has a depth of definitions, ranging from perceiving with sincerity to distinguishing and recognizing to the biblical sense of having intimate relations. *Learning* simply means to gain that knowledge—that awareness and insight that we can apply readily in our lives.

Learning and understanding certainly don't end when one graduates from school. Life is an ongoing classroom, and I don't know about anyone else, but my learning curve has been challenged a lot by emerging technologies and other socioeconomic transformations in our society. Quite honestly, I find it hard to keep up. When my mundane attempts to do so fail, I use the following instructions—or an adaptation of them—to help me cast a proverbial brain boost:

✦ Time your spells for when the moon is in Scorpio, Leo, or Taurus, Sundays, and bright days (the light of understanding).

✦ Add aromatics such as rosemary for
  memory retention or vanilla, marjoram,
  and mint for the conscious mind.

✦ Use yellow candles (to represent the Air
  Element, which governs our *thinking* self).

✦ Include other components and symbols such as
  glasses, notebooks, walnuts, amethyst, coral, and
  fluorite, all of which support successful learning
  and the effective applications of one's skills.

Spells

To make a learning charm, gather a yellow candle, an aromatic
of your choice, a small piece of paper (2 by 4 is good), and
your favorite pen. Light the candle and take a few minutes to
center yourself. Focus on your intention: the topic you hope to
comprehend more. Once you feel that your intention is fully
in focus, write the name of that topic on the paper. Pick up
the paper and speak the name therein so that your breath falls
across the sheet (breath gives life to energy). Finally, fold it
in half, in half again, and in half again (three times all told),
sealing it with wax as you might a letter. Keep this inside your
notebook or other study materials.

Make yourself a special *learning-understanding* candle
through the following steps. You'll need wax, a wick, aromatics
of your choice, some crushed coral, and a candle mold. You can
get nearly everything you need at a good hobby shop, and coral
can be crushed fairly easily using a rock to break it into smaller
pieces (wrap it in a cloth first so that you don't lose any).

Melt the wax, adding the aromatic chosen. Pour a little
of this into the bottom of the mold, sprinkling coral into the
foundation as you say:

The coral of wisdom, to my mind beckons.
As the light of the candle shines,
So, too, my understanding awakens.
Whenever this candle burns,
Improve my ability to learn!

Pour in the remaining wax and add the wick. (You can also save a little time by pouring the melted wax into a glass container that then becomes self-enclosed housing for the candle—meaning you won't need a holder.) After you release the candle from its mold, light it anytime you're sitting down to study (or learning something new) and keep it burning nearby.

Love

Of all the requests I get for help with spellcasting, Love Magic ranks the highest. I find this worrisome in one respect: love should not be manipulated, for when it is, the meaning is lost. Therefore, when I teach people love spells, I preface by asking them to think long and hard about what they want, what they need, and how to achieve those goals without manipulation (bearing in mind that what we *think* we need and what we truly need are often two different things). I submit the same advice to you along with one other thought: release your Love Magic to the world without necessarily focusing it on *one* person. When love comes back to you in any form, it is a blessing. Try not to put such a powerful and positive force into a preconceived box. You'll find your magic will respond in kind, and you will find interesting ways to bring and keep love in your life. To cast Love Magic:

+ Time your spells for the full moon (a very romantic time), when the moon is in Aquarius, or during the month of June.

✦ Add aromatics such as rose, apple, basil, cinnamon, lavender, lemon, orange, pine, and vanilla, all of which have established associations with love.

✦ Use pink or red candles (the darker the color, the deeper the level of intent).

✦ Include other components and symbols such as a heart or knots and crystals such as amethyst (peaceful love), amber, jade, lapis, and moonstone. Also, mead has long been considered a love and fertility philter (which is why it was a traditional honeymoon gift).

Spells

This first spell enhances already existing partnerships. Pick out a candle of the right color for your intention. Place a pin in the middle of the candle, focusing on your significant other. Light the candle, saying:

> *As this candle burns,*
> *Let my love be returned.*
> *If it be for the best,*
> *Then pray heed, my heart's request.*

(As you can see, this incantation provides a loophole: *if it be for the best.* Should your relationship be an unhealthy one, this incantation ensures that your magic won't feed the negativity.)

Let the candle burn until the pin falls out. You may use the remaining candle in other love spells.

This next spell focuses on bringing *new* love into your life. Spring is a good time to cast it—when the Earth itself is blossoming with hope. Pick out one candle to represent you. Surround it with eight other pink or red candles (again chosen for the intensity of the relationship desired).

This spell takes place over eight days, and I'd suggest starting as soon as the moon waxes out of the dark phase.

Pick out a time during which you can work consistently every night, undisturbed. Begin by lighting one candle and speaking your wishes into its flame. On night two, move the exterior candles a little closer to the candle that represents you and repeat this process with two candles. Continue in this manner until the eighth night, when the eight candles are nearly touching the *self* candle. Let them all naturally burn out, releasing your wishes to the universe.

If you want to improve a relationship (specifically the level of trust), pair this last spell with your mundane efforts. Begin with three candles—one to represent you, one for your heart, and one for your relationship as a whole—and three quartz crystals. Surround these with a combination of pink and green candles (green for growth and health). If possible, you should enact this spell with your significant other in a mini ritual that ensures their goals for your relationship are the same as yours.

Begin the spell at dawn each day for three days. On the first day, light your candle, look at your significant other, and share all that's in your heart and spirit. Put aside trivial issues and focus on all the goodness you have—all that you hope will come. On the second day, light your candle and have your significant other light theirs; this time, they'll share their joys, hopes, and dreams. Finally, on the third day, each of you lights your personal candle. From those two flames, ignite the relationship candle, repeating together:

> *In trust and love, blessed from above;*
> *As we carry this stone, our love to hone;*
> *In unity and harmony, we declare this spell is free!*

Leave the candles to burn and spend some quality time together. Each of you should always carry one of the three crystals with you, leaving the last one on your altar to represent your united minds and hearts.

Luck

I am willing to bet that if you randomly walked up to ten strangers and asked them if they wished they had more luck, the answer would be a resounding *yes!* Almost everyone I know (even those who are *naturally* a little lucky) could certainly use some more good fortune. When you feel like you've been plagued with ongoing red tape and barriers, when everything seems to be breaking or going wrong, or when you would just appreciate a lucky break, this flavor of Candle Magic can do the trick!

The only caution I have is that luck is a persnickety creature and often manifests in an odd form. For example, I was once working magic for luck in job-hunting, which resulted in several networking leads. This was great, but it created a ton of work, too! That's the way the Universe prefers to manifest—by bringing us the kind of luck no one can take away because we've helped create it with honest efforts.

To cast for luck:

+ Time your spells for when the sun is shining, the moon is in Pisces, spring mornings, or Sundays.

+ Add aromatics such as allspice, basil, heather, and nasturtium, all of which have fortunate energies.

+ Use your lucky color for the candle's hue.

✦ Include other components and symbols of luck such as dice and coins; edibles such as beans, corn, red rice, and kiwi; and stones such as jade, moonstone, tin, and carnelian.

Spells

This first spell requires a candle, some organic marigold petals, and water. To prepare, you'll need to simmer the marigolds in warm water until you get a tea-like infusion (one handful of marigold petals to one cup of water is fine). Add a little sugar to the tea, if you wish, to emphasize sweet fortune.

Next, light the candle with the cup of marigold tea nearby, saying:

> *As the light of hope shines,*
> *May good fortune be mine.*
> *And as I internalize this lucky tea,*
> *All good things shall come to me!*

Drink the tea completely, accepting its energy. Leave the candle (in a safe place) to burn itself out.

Find a large bay leaf—onto which you'll write the word *luck*. Take the candle of your lucky color and light it. Focus your intention of bringing good fortune to one specific area of your life. Light the bay leaf on the candle and place it in a fire-safe container to burn. As it releases smoke, use your hand to move the smoke upward toward the heavens, saying:

> *Higher and higher, my wish from the fire:*
> *Luck be kind, luck come quick.*
> *Luck released from this candle's wick!*

Once the bay leaf has burned out completely, take the remaining ashes outside and release them to the winds so that your wish is scattered to the Four Corners of creation. Blow out the candle and use it for other luck spells.

When you're having a streak of unusually bad luck, this next spell can help break that negativity. Wait until the moon is waning (you want to banish the bad fortune). Light a black candle and walk through your entire home counterclockwise. Stop in each room (or otherwise separate space) and recite the following incantation:

> *Into the darkness, away from light*
> *All ill will retreats, all bad fortune takes flight;*
> *Only goodness abounds, good luck surrounds.*

Afterward, break the black candle to symbolically *break* the hold of bad luck.

Magical Aptitude (Spirituality)

Magic is a methodology; spirituality is an ideology. In the context of this book, I have typically framed magic and spirituality as a cooperative effort because that is how it should be. I realize there are some readers who simply practice the art of magic without any particular ideology or philosophy behind it—as simply a tool. But because that's not how I live my life, I can't teach it that way!

I believe that a spirit or art that does not grow beyond its present state will wither and die as surely as a plant that doesn't reach out with roots for water. Allowing our magic to grow with personal and planetary transformations is essential. With that in mind, these candlelight spells endeavor to achieve a harmony of art and idea, then empower that partnership so that you can grow and advance on your path. They can also be used as a way of safeguarding yourself against ill-intended magic.

To harness magical aptitude:

+ Time your spells for when the moon is full, when the moon is in Pisces, or midnight (the Witching Hour).

+ Add aromatics such as carnation (power), lilac, sandalwood (magical aptitude and psychism), and lotus (spirituality).

+ Use a purple candle (for spiritual pursuits and wisdom) or a white candle (to represent the human spirit).

+ Include other components and symbols such as a bell, book, keys, any magical tools (such as a wand or athame), and rowan or willow wood.

Spells

There is an old European folk belief that a Witch's power resides in their hair. Building on this concept, take three strands of your hair and braid them together, saying:

> *Three by one, the spell is begun.*
> *Three by two, the power is true.*
> *Three by three, magic in me!*

Tie this braid around your chosen candle. Then, the next time you need to increase the energy of a spell, light it, and recite the incantation three times before enacting your spell or ritual. Leave the candle burning while you work.

Next, we'll go over a little household charm that's an adaptation of the anti-magic Witch Bottles people use to keep malevolent spells away. To begin, you'll need a flat-bottomed container, inside which you'll secure a black candle (to absorb negativity). Around the candle, place pieces of old, broken glass, rusted nails, or anything else sharp, gnarly, and reflective (to entangle or turn negative energy). You don't need a ton of these items, just enough so that the bottom of the container is covered. Leave this container near your hearth (a fireplace or stove) and light it whenever you feel a spell or ritual has raised energy against you (or whenever you feel psychically attacked).

This last spell serves as a fast way of creating sacred space to amplify your magic. For it, you need four candles—one red, one blue, one brown or green, and one yellow. Bless these candles, saying:

> *I charge you each, candles four,*
> *guard well, safeguard magic's door.*
> *As Watchtowers and Guides pure,*
> *all unwanted influences deter,*
> *And with this flame I now ignite,*
> *the power in this spell takes to flight!*

Put these candles as close as possible to the Four Directional Quarters in your home or magical workroom. Light them just before enacting any magic for which you'd like both a sacred space and an energy boost. You can use the same incantation to turn on their energy should you wish—or use another invocation of your own for the Elements.

Meditation

Plenty of people have trouble meditating. If you fall into this category, don't feel bad. It's normal for the human mind to want to juggle multiple concepts and tasks at the same time. However, meditation asks you to focus on one area and one problem—or to simply release yourself from thinking long enough to destress. Meditation can actually bring down your blood pressure! In this section, we'll examine a candlelight meditation and spell, both of which are aimed at improving the overall meditation experience so that you get the desired results. You'll need to:

+ Time your spells for dusk or evening (darkness seems to improve the effect for most people) or during the full moon (for improved insight).

+ Add aromatics such as sandalwood, lotus, and sweetgrass, all of which are used to create a highly charged atmosphere for internal workings.

+ Use a blue or white candle.

+ Include other components and symbols such as amethyst, fluorite, and silver (all of which accent the meditative process). Also consider chimes or a drumbeat to help center your mind and thoughts.

Spells

For this first activity, you'll need a small drum—or any object that can act as a drum, such as an overturned bowl—and a blue candle. Think about the things in your life that require some serious contemplation. Pick out one topic for this meditation and carve a symbol (or words) representing that topic into the candle. Focus wholly on your intent to broaden your perspective on that topic (or whatever other insights you need).

Next, light the candle. Put your hands, palms down, on the drum's surface and breathe deeply. Listen closely for the sound of your heartbeat. Mirror that rhythm on the drum, focusing on both the sound and your intention. Once the beat becomes natural, allow images of the topic at hand to form in your mind. Don't try to hold them or force them. You will remember them afterward, so just let go and allow your mind, heart, and spirit to work cooperatively.

When the images cease, or you start losing your ability to concentrate, stop drumming and write down some notes about your experience. Read them over once or twice while the candle still burns so it can illuminate your understanding. Then, blow out the candle and keep it for other meditative moments.

In many traditions, meditation need not be something that's still. There are walking meditations and even dancing meditations. We live in a highly mobile society, so this idea holds a lot of merit. The purpose of this next bit of magic is to make a charm you can carry during your moving meditations.

Begin with a candle, some lotus oil, and a crystal of your choice. Light the candle. Hold the stone in your non-dominant hand and, using your dominant hand, dab it with a bit of oil. Rub this in as if you're using the crystal as a worry stone, but stay focused on your intention of making the stone a cue for moving meditations. If you wish, add an incantation such as:

Focus be born, distraction abate;
Help me as I meditate.

Place a drop or two of wax on the stone and wrap it in a soft cloth. Carry this with you when you take walks or try other forms of moving meditation. If you can touch the stone periodically (especially when you feel distracted), it improves the results.

Memory

We have a saying in my house: "If it's not written down, it does not exist." This has come about due to my propensity for writing lists and notes and leaving them everywhere so that I remember everything that needs to be done. Without them, I fear my life would fall into chaos. But what about the times when there's no paper available or strings to tie around your finger? Or the times when you need to be certain of remembering important things without any prop or prompting (such as your lines for a wedding ritual or the date of your anniversary)? Candlelight memory spells and charms aim to shine a light into the corners of your mind where that information is stored (but where it also sometimes seems to hide, out of reach). To cast for enhanced memory:

+ Time your spells for the daylight hours (if trying to remember *conscious mind* items) or moonlit nights (for more esoteric memorization)— particularly when the moon is in Aries.

+ Add aromatics such as rosemary, apple, vanilla, and coffee, all of which strengthen the mind.

+ Use a yellow candle.

+ Include other components and symbols such as mustard seed, quartz crystals (for clarity), a memory chip from a computer, or knots (to hold the learning).

Spells

I like to combine memory spells with something portable simply because I usually need to remember something when I do *not* have access to a fast reference. The two spells I'm sharing here are constructed with that kind of situation in mind (rather like magically tying a string around your finger).

This first one requires a quartz crystal and a candle. Take the quartz outside under the bright sunshine to absorb the energy. In a nearby area, light the candle. Speak all the information or tasks that you need to remember into the crystal and the flame of the candle. When you're done doing this, drop a bit of candle wax on the crystal, saying:

As sure as wax from this flame,
Remembrance I claim;
When held to my brain,
The memories retain;
When held to my heart,
Your information impart!

Following the pattern of the spell, hold the crystal to your forehead and recite your list of information again, then tuck it in your pocket. Put the crystal to your heart when you sense you're forgetting something.

The second spell begins as the first, but this time, you need a length of yellow ribbon or yarn and a candle. Light the candle and look over the materials you need to remember by the warmth of its light. Next, take up the length of ribbon or yarn and tie those pieces of information to it by speaking each one into the strand and making a knot, then adding:

Bound within, the spell brings;
When unwound, memory abounds!

Repeat this process all the way down the length of the yarn or ribbon. You can make your list as long or short as you want, but don't try to cram too much information into each knot. Just like a mundane knot, it can only house so much pressure. Typically, I put one factoid or chore in each knot. Taking this one step further, I sometimes color-code the knots using a marker (brown for a household chore, yellow for a birthday, and so on). That way, when I realize I can't remember, I can undo the knot that releases the correct information.

An alternative to this would be to make a general memory Witch's ladder (the length of knots is called that by tradition). Use the very same incantation when tying the knots, but don't focus on any specific type of information. Dab these knots with some rosemary oil and open one at a time as needed. Just don't open the last knot! When the strand gets down to one, recharge it with fresh magic and new knots.

Money

Just as with health, happiness, and luck, money is one of those things that we need and of which we often wish we had more. My mother told me that money doesn't buy happiness, but it makes it a lot easier! I agree. While there's a difference between greed and need, I see no reason not to utilize magic to help us prosper so that we can focus a little more time on family, friends, and our spiritual lives.

As with other touchy ethical issues, the results from Money Magic can be quite surprising. Typically, when I ask for money, I am given extra work through which to make that money. I see this in other people's lives, too, almost as a universal means of checks and balances that keep us honest! So be prepared to roll up your sleeves:

+ Time your spells for when the moon is in Aquarius or Pisces, a blue moon, Sundays, New Year's, or any day in spring (for growth-oriented energies).

+ Add aromatics such as cedar, dill, vetiver, almond, basil, cinnamon, orange, nutmeg, and woodruff.

+ Use green, silver, or gold candles (green for paper money, silver for smaller amounts, and gold for larger amounts).

✦ Include other components and symbols such as
a dollar sign, rice, moss agate, alfalfa, piggy banks,
and your wallet.

Spells

Collect a wide-based candle in the color of your choice, a
silver or gold coin (preferably one minted in the year of your
birth), and some high-quality olive oil (an old Italian charm
for prosperity). Perform the actual working anytime between
the waxing and full moon for growth-oriented energies.

Begin by warming the bottom of your candle just enough
to press the coin into it (you want money at the foundation
of the candle's energy). When that's secure, dress the candle
in olive oil, moving clockwise with your fingers upward from
the base of the candle. Focus wholly on your intent to improve
the overall flow of money in your home.

Next, at dawn each morning, light the candle and say:

As the candle glows
And wax flows,
Let money grow.

Continue until the moon is in the second day of fullness,
then hold on to the candle for the following month. If you
wish, keep your wallet or checkbook nearby when enacting the
spell and carry a bit of the wax remnants as a money charm.

This next spell is a good one to enact on New Year's, but
it can be done anytime family and friends are present. Have
everyone contribute some loose change to a clear container.
Put this on a table. Next, take one candle for each person
present and surround the jar completely. Those who wish to
participate should light their own candles and take one coin
each from the jar to leave near their personal tapers. As they
remove their coins, they should think of the amount of money

they truly need (not *want*, but really need). Once everyone has done this, join hands and chant together:

> *Restrictions decrease.*
> *Money increase.*
> *In the light of the flame,*
> *Our wishes, we claim.*

Continue to repeat this until your voices rise and naturally crescendo. At this point, break hands and lift them upward to send the magic on its way. Each person keeps their coin and candle (the coin as a money charm and the candle for money magic at home). The rest of the jar should be used for a charitable purpose.

Movement

Movement is tied in with the course and process of change. It is not simply about getting from here to there but about both literal and figurative transformations that provide some kind of progress in a specific direction. So, when you feel like you're spinning your wheels and need a spiritual tow truck, these candlelight spells and charms offer that kind of anchor. They can also help you when you're facing a choice or challenge and feel frozen in your tracks because of its difficulty. To cast for movement:

+ Time your spells for right after the dark moon (when everything starts moving forward again) or the season of spring.

+ Add energetic aromatics such as ginger, carnation, vanilla, marigold, or thyme.

✦ Use a candle whose color represents the area of your life that seems to be stagnating or moving too slowly.

✦ Include other components and symbols that have some type of action to them, such as kinetic toys, pinwheels, and so on. You want to visually put the magic into motion to mirror your intention.

Spells

For this first spell, you'll need a candle into which you've carved an emblem representing the area of your life where the need exists. You'll also need a children's pinwheel, a small paintbrush, and a magic marker. Write a word that describes your need on each of the pinwheel's sections. Lay it aside.

Next, melt the candle in a non-aluminum pan until the carved emblem disappears. Use the paintbrush to apply a very light coating of the wax over the word you've written on the pinwheel as you say:

> *Hear my prayer, hear my request;*
> *By my will, this spell manifests;*
> *Change, unfold—the powers behoove;*
> *With life's breath, things start to move!*

Now, focus wholly on your need and blow on the pinwheel to put it into motion. If you can leave it outside to let the winds help spiral the energy, all the better. Save your wax

for any type of spell that requires a little manifesting energy.

This next spell is designed to take place over the span of at least a week (longer if necessary). First, you need to get a good number of self-enclosed candles (the large ones are available in many different stores as prayer candles). If it's possible, get them in rainbow colors, arranging them from red to violet so that the color of the candle progresses forward—similar to how you want other things to move forward.

Starting on the first day of a waxing moon, light the candle, saying:

> *The first light burns and shall not go out.*
> *It is my wish—my heart's desire.*

This candle should be kept burning continuously until the next night. At that time, you can use a twig or a long-handled match to light the second candle from the flame of the first. (If you need to replace any candles during this process because they gave out, always light the replacement from the original to illustrate the continuation of energy.) As you light the second candle, say:

> *The first light burns;*
> *it is my wish—my heart's desire;*
> *The second light burns true,*
> *supporting the first, bringing light in the darkness.*

Follow this same pattern for the seven days (or however long you choose to cast this spell), repeating the incantation to the line that corresponds with the day:

Day 1:

> *The first light burns, It is my wish—my heart's desire.*

Day 2:

> *The second light burns true,*
> *supporting the first,*
> *Bringing light to the darkness.*

Day 3:

> *The third light burns in me,*
> *Giving me the hope and power to keep trying.*

Day 4:

> *The fourth light burns,*
> *Guiding energy toward my goal.*

Day 5:

> *The fifth light burns,*
> *Overcoming any blockages.*

Day 6:

> *The sixth light burns,*
> *And the wheel of time turns.*

Day 7:

> *The seventh light shines,*
> *What I wish is mine!*

Let these burn out naturally after the seventh candle.

Networking

> *There are two ways of spreading light:*
> *to be the candle or the mirror that reflects it.*
> —Edith Wharton

Word of mouth is still the best way to go about getting good information from those who have *been there* and *done that*. Among Neo-Pagans, networking has been elevated to a new art. We've depended on it heavily for a great deal of things, ranging from finding teachers to locating a decent organic herbal shop. What happens, however, when your normal web-weaving contacts come up empty-handed? That's the ideal time to pull out a little magic:

+ Time your spells for dusk (networking requires
  a balance of rational and intuitive thought, and
  dusk often allows for both sunlight and moonlight
  to appear). Alternatively, wait until the moon
  is in Virgo to encourage fruitful alliances.

+ Add aromatics such as lemon (for
  networking with friends), heather (for a
  little luck), and ginger (for success).

+ Use a white candle (because you never know what
  form your networking contacts may take).

+ Include other components and symbols such
  as webs (or string), carnelian or beryl (for
  effective communication), Eastern winds (to
  carry your missives), and a telephone.

Spells

This activity uses a candle and string (as a type of pendulum)
to help you find contacts in a specific area of a map. Begin by
securing the candle with the length of string; this will allow
you to hold the candle upside down over the map with your
elbow securely on the table (but off of the map). Think about
your networking questions as you tie the knot in place, saying:

> *A web to weave, a(n) (object of search) to find;*
> *In wax, now leave a trail behind!*

Fill in the blank with what you're looking for (a coven, a
New Age store, or the like). If you find that the thread slips off
the candle, you can use some melted wax from a second one to
hold it secure. Now, light the candle and suspend it carefully

about five inches above the surface of the map. Steady the unlit end with your other hand. Again, focus on your question and repeat the incantation eight times slowly. Try not to look directly at the map; you don't want to accidentally skew this divination effort (your hand will often follow eye movement). When you're done, blow out the candle and see what patterns or areas the wax dripped on.

This next spell is similar to the first, but this time, you'll need about two feet of cotton thread (any color), a picture of a spider web, and your candle. Put the image of the web under the candle (the foundation for the magic) on a fire-safe surface. Now, lay the candle at the center point of the cotton thread and crisscross the thread upward from the bottom of the candle, tying a knot at each crossed point and saying:

> *Grandmother spider, teacher of words,*
> *Weave your web in my life; let my prayer be heard,*
> *One to one, one to three, exponentially out from me,*
>
> *Thread to thread, mind to mind, help me with*
> *A(n) (object of search) to find.*

(You can fill in the blank with the same networking need at each knot or different needs.)

Set the candle upright on the image and light it. When the candle burns a knot open, it releases its magic.

Oaths (Promises)

An oath or vow is a kind of magic unto itself. Those of a metaphysical persuasion, however, like to bring a more ritualistic overtone to such moments and reinforce our promises with a spiritual commitment. This comes from the understanding that a promise is not simply a bundle of words

—it's intention, which is also at the heart of magic. No matter how good our intentions may be, some promises are very hard to keep, so supporting them with a little extra energy makes sense. To do so:

✦ Time your spells for when the moon is in Libra (for equity), Tuesdays (if making a legal commitment), or Fridays (for relationship promises).

✦ Add aromatics such as lilac (harmony), magnolia (peace and devotion), and myrrh (protection).

✦ Use a white candle for pure motivation.

✦ Include other components and symbols such as bluebell or eyebright (to determine honest intent), agate (for blessing the promise), cups, and knots.

Spells

This first activity is designed specifically for the promise made between a couple, either for an engagement, handfasting, wedding, or similar commitment. For it, you'll need several feet of deep red, pink, and white yarn, some rose oil, and a white candle. Carve a heart (or other symbol representing your promise) into the candle. Light it and sit nearby as you braid the yarn, chanting:

> *Two hearts, true hearts from us both,*
> *Braided three by three, let us honor our oath!*

When the braid is complete, wax both ends so that it doesn't come undone, then blow out the candle. There are several ways you can use this strand at this point. It can become the handfasting cloth for binding the couple's hands at the end of the ritual, or you can wrap the strand around the candle and store it in a safe place to protect the commitment made.

This next charm is for people who find they sometimes have trouble fulfilling the commitments they make. Begin with a candle, two eye agates, a three-by-three cloth, and a string. Light the candle and focus on your intent: to be more dependable (or not to overextend yourself). Put the two eye agates in the center of the cloth, saying:

> *Eyes of spirit, eyes of mind,*
> *In this pouch, my magic bind.*
> *A promise to keep, a promise once made,*
> *From my mind, it never fades.*

Drip a little candle wax into the center of the cloth, then bundle it with the string. Keep this with you whenever you're juggling a lot of different responsibilities.

Opportunity

No one wants to be in the middle of the desert when their ship finally comes in. I myself always seem to be away from home when opportunity finally knocks. To avoid these types of situations and open up more opportunity in all areas of your life, try out the following and see what kind of chances come your way:

+ Time your spells for dawn, spring (the time of openings and awakenings), during the waxing to full moon, or when the moon is in Taurus.

+ Add aromatics such as apple, nutmeg, and vanilla.

+ Use a candle whose color represents the area of your life in which the opportunity is needed (for work, you might use brown or green to stress the Earth Element).

+ Include other components and symbols such as doors, keys, windows, bridges, and can openers (all of which imply some type of opening or movement).

Spells

This first activity requires an outdoor container—such as a lantern—to house your chosen candles (so you can still burn them if it rains). You'll also need seven candles and an aromatic that best represents your goal. Dab this lantern with your chosen aromatic, then carve an image of that goal into the wax of each candle. During the next week, take one candle outside your house each morning at dawn and light it, saying:

As the sun brings a new day, so too open the way;
Hear my prayer, and to me, bring many more openings!

Leave the candle to burn while you go about your tasks. Bring it in at dusk. Repeat over the full seven days, each day with a fresh candle. Keep your eyes and ears open for opportunity's knock.

Using the wax from the last activity and an old key, you can make yourself a portable opportunity charm. Warm the wax by rubbing it between your hands until it gets soft enough to shape around the key. As you form it to the key, chant something like:

Magic, saturate this little key,
Bring to me opportunity!

Keep repeating the phrase until the key is enclosed in the wax, then carry it with you regularly. If you're ever in a situation where you need a very fast response, take the key out of the wax and say:

> *Unlock the magic in my key,*
> *By my will, the spell is free!*

This last activity uses candle drippings (as a type of divination) to help you pinpoint where an opportunity might lie out of a variety of possibilities. Say you have several potential jobs for which to apply and want to limit your choices to the best ones—print out those online listings or gather the business cards. Lay them out randomly on a piece of craft paper (face down).

Next, light a yellow candle (for communication and messages). Concentrate on your goal of choosing the right jobs. Hold that candle in your dominant hand, and without looking at the pieces of paper, mix them up with your free hand. Now, hold the candle over the surface (don't look down—you don't want to skew the reading) and repeat this incantation four times:

> *My efforts and focus, pray direct;*
> *Let my choices be correct!*

(*Four* is an Earth number that correlates with Job-Oriented Magic; obviously, if your networking goal is different, change the number of repetitions.)

Finally, look at the listings or cards that the wax landed on and begin there.

Organization

Organization is not a four-letter word! Having everything in order has many advantages. In the Eastern system of feng shui (the art of placement), orderliness (over clutter) opens the flow of beneficial energy in any space. Similarly, in metaphysical traditions, organization provides a framework within which everything flows more smoothly. Unfortunately, maintaining a tidy composition or ordered methodology aren't personal traits that come easily or naturally to many people. And while you'll have to continue to make efforts on a mundane level to develop those aptitudes, there's no reason not to look for spiritual support, too. So:

+ Time your spells for noon (to emphasize rational, orderly thought), spring-cleaning time, when the moon is in Leo, or Sundays.

+ Add aromatics that strengthen the conscious mind, such as rosemary, apple, and almond.

+ Use a gold or vibrant orange candle.

+ Include other components and symbols such as a notepad, a palm organizer, a calculator, cleaning implements, or a filing cabinet. Also try Fire-oriented stones (to put a fire under those projects), such as red agate and amber.

Spells
For this first activity, all you'll need is a gold candle dabbed with a chosen aromatic and a little undisturbed time. Sit comfortably in front of the candle and light it. Breathe deeply

and relax. Watch the candle until you can see it clearly in your mind's eye, then close your eyes.

Next, visualize the flame of the candle growing larger until it surrounds you. Let this saturate your entire aura until it glows with a golden hue. If you can see the light like a patterned matrix (geometric), all the better—patterns represent order. When you feel yourself growing warm from this exercise, change your perspective slightly and imagine the area of your life that needs to be put in order. Surround it with the same patterned energy glow. Continue until you feel that energy has fixed itself in place (this is hard to describe, but you'll just *know* when it happens).

Return to normal awareness, take your candle into the respective area of your life, and get busy!

In this next activity, you can prepare a nice edible treat to eat in the light of your energized candle. Take one apple and slice it. Fry it lightly in butter and rosemary (go light on the rosemary). Stir the mix clockwise in the pan—to work with sun energy—and say:

> *Apple for wisdom and spice for my mind,*
> *Within this food, ordered magic combines!*

Keep repeating the incantation while you cook. Then, sit down with a lit candle and let the light of motivation shine on your food. Repeat the incantation silently in your mind while you consume the apple. Eating internalizes the energy you've created.

This last spell takes place over three days. Start by putting any four candles you happen to have handy out on a surface so that they're scattered. Each day at dawn, light the candles and say:

> *Out of darkness comes light.*

147

Then move the candles slightly so that they're closer to being in a tidy line, saying:

Out of chaos comes order.

Repeat this each day for the next three days (making sure the candles are lined up perfectly on the third day). If you can leave them in that area and light them only when you feel like you're getting disorganized, that's a great support system for the spell. If not, however, just let the candles burn naturally out.

Overcoming

I continue to create because writing is a labor of love and also an act of defiance, a way to light a candle in a gale wind.
—Alice Childress

How many times have you felt like a situation was impossible? When you're faced with overwhelming odds, continual setbacks, a habit you can't seem to break, or the proverbial brick wall without a dent in sight, it's time to pull a little positive energy out of your Candle Magic kit. These spells are designed to give you a little more luck, personal fortitude, or a leg up when you need one most. You'll want to:

+ Time your spells for the waning to dark moon (so that obstacles shrink) or when the moon is in Aries (breaks down barriers) or Scorpio (reverses negatives).

+ Add aromatics such as borage (courage), bay leaves (strength), and cinnamon (success).

✦ Use a red-colored candle (the fire Element,
which provides both burning energy and
the capacity to destroy obstacles).

✦ Include other components and symbols, such
as items that loosen or open (to likewise shake
matters loose or create new openings).

Spells

This first activity uses a candle of your choosing and an image
of the obstacle you face. Make sure the image is something
that combusts easily. For example, if you are having trouble
getting money, a picture of a dollar bill behind a door (or in a
box) might work. You'll also want a fire-safe container where
it can burn out completely.

Light your candle and hold your image in your dominant
hand, bringing to mind the circumstances that frustrate you.
Move the image to the flame and say:

Barriers be broken, let the way be open.

When the image catches fully, transfer it carefully to the
container, continuing to chant while it burns. Watch as the
obstacle is literally destroyed before your eyes. When the
flames are gone, blow out the candle and bury the ashes so
that something positive can come of the momentary delays
you've experienced. Keep the candle for other similar spells
(such as success and victory).

This next visualization uses a candle as a prop; you can
certainly bring it into your private sacred space to improve the
effect of the activity. Begin by getting comfortable in a chair
with your chosen candle in front of you. Light the candle so
you can keep a strong image of how it looks in your mind's
eye. Slowly release all tension within you and breathe deeply.

When you feel centered, direct your mind to making an imaginary paper wall—in front of which you're standing astrally. On that wall, you'll find images of everything you feel is presently holding you back. The images to the left are of things you had to overcome in the past; those in front are from the present, and those to the right are still forming but represent future obstacles.

Now, with faith and determination, take your mental candle—which came with you into the visualization—and burn the barrier away. When it is completely ash, take another deep breath and dissipate all that negativity completely to the wind. Return to normal awareness. Make note of any interesting experiences that happened during (or after) the visualization.

Passion (Lust)

Sometimes, you need to spark a fire. Other times, you need to give it a little boost to burn brightly. And still *other* times, when an interested party is a little too interested, you need to put that fire out! Whatever the case, when our amorous physical nature isn't cooperating the way we wish, it provides us with an opportunity to apply a little positive Candle Magic directly to our love lives:

+ Time your spells for when the sun is shining (blessings), the full moon (a very romantic time), when the moon is in Scorpio, and on May Day.

+ Add lustful aromatics such as cinnamon, hibiscus, mint, vanilla, and violet.

+ Use deep red candles (to light the fires within).

✦ Include other components and symbols that are known to inspire passion. Among foodstuffs, there's asparagus, banana, carrot, orange, fish, cucumbers, and eggs; for crystals, turn to those that have a vibrant red hue, such as red agates and red jasper.

Spells

Rather than use a candle as the main component in this first spell, let's consider using it as additional ambiance to set the mood for a mutually enjoyed passion potion. Begin with three cups of orange juice in a blender, about 1/2 of a banana, and a hint of vanilla extract. Whip this to froth, saying:

> *Round and round, burning desire,*
> *Take our passions ever higher!*

Pour the potion into a cup (to unite your purpose with that of your partner) and drizzle with a little melted chocolate and sweet cream. Serve by candlelight, drink fully, and let Nature take her course.

For this next activity, you're going to make a special passion candle that you or your significant other can light as a signal that you're in the mood. Begin with red wax and a mold of your choice (I think something with sensual overtones would be apt, but a lot here depends on what kind of decor you have around the house). In the base of the candle, place two red stones to represent each of you. Mingle whatever passionate aromatics you both like into the wax while it's cooling. Stir clockwise as you say:

> *Two hearts, one flame—our passion reclaim.*

Continue to whisper this incantation into the wax until it's ready to be put in the mold. Use the incantation again each time you light the candle to unlock your magic.

Sometimes, we may want to cool down a relationship that's getting overheated. To accomplish this, take a candle that represents the overly interested person, dab it with their favorite aromatic, and carve their name into it. On each night from the waning to dark moon, light the candle, saying:

> *Let (name)'s passion grow gentle and calm*
> *If it be their will, and it do no harm.*

This incantation does not manipulate the individual but rather offers a cooling energy that they can accept or reject. However, I do suggest that—after completing the spell—you place the candle in the freezer temporarily and go have a serious conversation with said individual, explaining how their continued lustful behavior may negatively impact the relationship you have with them.

Rites of Passage

> *Out, out, brief candle!*
> *Life's but a walking shadow, a poor player That struts*
> *and frets his hour upon the stage And then is heard no more.*
> —William Shakespeare, *Macbeth*

Nearly every important moment in human life has been commemorated somehow through rituals and mini rituals. Rites of Passage are among the most important of these commemorations because they earmark our lives' important transitions: birth, adulthood, eldership, and death. For the living, Rites of Passage provide an important opportunity to integrate our experiences and feelings. For the dead, they honor memories and send off the souls with good wishes on their journeys.

As with holidays, the size of this book doesn't allow for an extensive exploration of every Rite of Passage. I can, however, provide a list of suggestions on utilizing candles and aromatics for several. This is only a basic foundation—to which you'll add your knowledge of the individual for whom the ritual is being performed. Talk to them about what they want, making note of what might be meaningful and memorable to them. Get friends and family involved. If you surround the sacred space with love and thoughtfulness, you can't go wrong!

Birth

Although we enter this life with our past lives imprinted on our spirit, the newborn child is pure. A white candle, therefore, is appropriate. In terms of aromatics, please be careful. Some newborns can have negative reactions to aromas, so keep them light. I suggest simmering a potpourri blend of lily of the valley and other white flowers to represent innocence.

Adulthood

Because the child is about to take on an adult role in your household (and possibly at your Circle), let them pick out the candles and aromatics they prefer. Ask them to think about the significance of each and share it with you so you can integrate that meaning into the words of the ritual. In terms of timing, many young people partake of this ritual when they have their first menses; otherwise, the ritual typically takes place between the ages of thirteen and eighteen, with the average being at age sixteen.

First Home Away from Home

Typically, one's college years are an excellent time to make a house candle that represents the spirit of a new home, encouraging joy and peace within. The person living in the new house should make the candle (the color being their choice), but if they wish, they can form it from remnants of family and friends' candles to inspire warm feelings.

Wedding or Handfasting

This is a very important Rite of Passage that implies a unity of heart and spirit. One of the most common types of candle symbolism used at these rituals is that of two candles lighting one central candle to honor that *oneness*. Another lovely addition to late afternoon weddings is candlelit processional areas—to illuminate the way toward a new life together.

Eldership

When I think of the strongly grounded characteristics of an elder, the first color that comes to mind is brown, such as the color of soil that's accepted the sun and rain and has been enriched. For aromatics, ask if the person has a god or goddess that they follow, then apply aromatics that honor that deity.

Death

Rites of Passage for the dead are designed to help the soul's transition and to provide a coping mechanism for those left behind. In this rite, I suggest using a white candle to represent the deity and a candle whose color is chosen based on the deceased's favorite hue. Aromatics should be peaceful (such as lavender) or those that somehow celebrate that person's life (such as their favorite incense, perfume, or cologne). As with all other candle-lighting efforts, don't overlook the importance of your intention as you place flame to wick. Also, don't forget to trust your instincts and allow for moments of inspired magic.

Peace (and Quiet)

Our lives are literally inundated with sound. Honking horns, barking dogs, crying children, blaring radios—these things and many others intrude on our day nearly non-stop. This is so much the case that it's no wonder we have trouble hearing the still, small voice of Spirit—They can't get a word in edgewise! This constant level of noise and commotion tends to leave people feeling out of sorts and restless (and often not knowing exactly why).

The beauty of metaphysics is that when a spell or ritual is enacted correctly, it can (and does) affect the temporal realm. In this case, you'll be using your magic to set up an astral barrier between you and the source of noise or disruption so that some semblance of peace is restored. To do so:

+ Time your spells for the waning moon, when the moon is in Libra, or dawn (for hope of a better start).

+ Add harmonious aromatics such as gardenia, lavender, myrtle, pennyroyal, and violet.

+ Use a white candle (to signal a truce and pure intention).

+ Include other components and symbols such as a white flag, willow wood (adaptive energy), amethyst (for self-control and improved serenity), or anything else that you associate with reclaiming tranquility.

Spells
To encourage peace in a specific situation or between yourself and another person, you can turn your candle into a poppet. To achieve the greatest effect, I'd suggest a black candle to

155

represent ire or negativity. From the last night of the full moon until the dark moon, light the candle and say:

> *Hostilities cease;*
> *I reclaim peace!*

Continuously recite the incantation for a few minutes, directing all the negative energy associated with that situation into the candle. On the last night of this activity, let the wax burn out completely. After the wax cools, break it into tiny pieces (likewise breaking up the energy stored within) and dispose of it properly.

This next activity provides a magical means of opening the way for peace between people. In this case, I'm going to suggest you use the energy of a waxing moon to infuse the situation with positivity. Also, put the candles in a somewhat sunny location while you're burning them (to balance the emotional self with more rational thought).

Begin with one candle for each person involved in the dispute. Place these around a white central candle to represent the Spirit of Peace and Understanding. Each day, move the candles slightly closer to each other, then light them from the Spirit candle, saying:

> *We come together joined by the Light of Spirit;*
> *We grow closer to understanding, illuminated by wisdom;*
> *We reach for peace and renewal*
> *With the spark of honorable intent;*
> *We seek healing in the glow of mutual respect.*
> *So be it.*

On the final night of working (which should be the second night of the full moon before it begins to shrink), let the candles burn out naturally, then make your calls or go for a visit. See what opportunities Spirit makes for reconciliation.

I don't know about the rest of you, but it seems every person who knows me waits until the worst possible moment to call, visit, or have a need. There are times when all of us want to be left undisturbed, be it for magic or a decent nap. With this in mind, this last activity is meant to encourage calm and quiet.

Take a white candle into the room where you want to create the sphere of silence. Light it in the Eastern part of that room and begin walking the entire perimeter (clockwise to draw silence, counterclockwise to banish noise), visualizing the glow of the candle extending outward to the walls, windows, doors, ceiling, air ducts, and electrical outlets—everything in sight awash with light like a huge glowing bubble. Take up a comfortable spot in the center of that bubble and remain as long as you wish. Just note that once the candle goes out, the energy field dissipates fairly quickly.

Power

Has the spark in your wand fizzled out? Do you feel like every ritual or spell has a damper on it, and the energy goes nowhere? Ever get the sense that you have absolutely no power to transform a specific situation? Each of these examples is a perfect reason to pull out some candlepower! You'll want to:

+ Time your spells for summer (especially the Summer Solstice), the full moon (for both rational and intuitive power), Tuesdays (strength), when the moon is in Scorpio (Fiery energy), or when the overall ambient temperature outside is slowly rising.

✦ Add aromatics such as chrysanthemum, carnation, and ginger.

✦ Use red candles (or bright purple for power balanced with wisdom).

✦ Include other components and symbols such as batteries, a bell (to center the energy), hair (a Witch's power is said to reside here), and a wand or athame (both used to direct magical energy and power).

Spells

We'll start with a generalized power ritual that you can use to saturate yourself or any item you wish with energy. For the best results, I suggest enacting it at dawn on the Summer Solstice. You'll need a candle (or as many candles as you wish—this is a Fire festival) and four flowering seeds.

Begin by finding a spot where you can easily see the sunrise and where you have a flat surface on which to rest the candle. While you're waiting for the sun to rise, toss the seeds toward the Four Directions (one each) and say:

Guardian of the East, empower my communication.
Guardian of the South, energize my conscious mind.
Guardian of the West, spark my emotions and psychic self.
Guardian of the North, illuminate my foundations.

Now, wait until you see the very first glimmers peeking across the horizon. Welcome them as you light the candle, saying:

Sun reaching over the heights,
Fill me with power and light.

Spend as much time here as you wish absorbing the sun's

warmth. Then, leave any tools you've brought to charge until you return home.

While power has a strong Fire Element overtone, the moon's symbolism can be used to encourage it as well, especially in metaphysical matters. In this next ritual, you'll be engaging in a similar process as before, only on each night of the full moon as it first appears in the sky.

Take your candle outside and light it as the moonlight reaches the Earth, saying:

> *As the silvery beams and flames glow,*
> *As above, so below,*
> *Power I wish for, power I'll know.*

On the last night, sit in the light of the moon and the candle, taking notes for your magical grimoire or writing down any insights you receive about power and the wise use thereof.

When you need to *plug in* on the road (it's not always possible to find a private outdoor location), you can use a charm you've brought with you—and here's how you make it! On any convenient Tuesday, light a red candle and focus on your goal. Take an AA or AAA battery (fully charged) and wrap a strand of your hair around it. Drip some wax on the hair (to keep it in place), saying:

> *By this Witch's hair and battery,*
> *I hereby claim energy.*
> *The spell held true by candle wick,*
> *And with my will, the charm affix.*

Carry this with you when you know you'll be away from home for a while and may need a little extra energy. The charm works best if you hold it in your hand and recite the incantation to yourself. If the hair ever falls off, you'll need to remake the charm.

Protection

Plenty of people cast protection spells or enact safety rituals only *after* something has gone awry. I would recommend being a little more proactive than that. Our world is full of hazards. Heck, just getting out of bed can be tricky if you have children or pets who litter your floors with toys! Those who live in urban environments have the additional cumulative negativity of stressed-out people with which to cope. This is even more reason to regularly engage in protective Candle Magic; it'll serve as a spiritual vitamin to keep you safe and sound. To cast for protection:

+ Time your spells for when the moon is in Aries (cleansing) or Virgo (success), during hours of bright sunlight to banish the shadows, or during the entire month of January (shielding energy).

+ Add aromatics such as basil, cedar, hawthorn flowers, and woodruff flowers.

+ Use a white candle (for Spirit and the white light of protection).

+ Include other components and symbols associated with protection, such as eye agates, ash wood, bells, a Witch jar, cat's eye, drums, garlic, knots (to bind negativity), and the color red (which is considered abhorrent to ghosts and malicious fairies).

Spells
Candles make for a lovely visual symbol of the protective white light of which we speak. For this first activity, you'll need an object that represents the person or situation that

needs protection. Then, gather plenty of white candles so that they surround the symbolic item with an inward spiral of light energy (you want to direct the candlepower *toward* the object, not away from it).

Light these candles at dusk every night and leave them burning for a few minutes while you direct prayers or invocations on behalf of said person or situation. Continue until you know for certain that any potential harm has passed. Afterward, if you wish, melt the remaining candle wax and make a shielding candle for that person (or, to place in an area significant to that situation); this can then be lit if any issues resurface.

Speaking of shielding candles, a simple way to protect your home is by designing special room candles. I suggest having four, each in the color of one of the Elements (yellow for East and Air, red for South and Fire, blue or purple for West and Water, and green or brown for North and Earth). Prior to putting these around your house, leave them wrapped for a few weeks in a soft cloth that's been dabbed with frankincense, pine, and sage oil. The wax will absorb the aroma, but it won't be overwhelming.

After the candles have been scented, place each in its appropriate Elemental Quarter. Add an invocation so that when you light the candles, they create a semi-formal sacred space without fuss. Here's one example:

Guardian of the East and Air, protect this space
When your wick flares. (Light the Air candle.)

Guardian of the South and Fire, protect this space
When your flame grows higher. (Light the Fire candle.)

Guardian of the West and Water, protect this space

161

And never let the light falter. (Light the Water candle.)

Guardian of the North and Earth, protect this space
When your sparks give birth. (Light the Earth candle.)

Guardians in my sacred space give shelter
In all storms. (Stand in center.)

No negativity is welcome here, and none may harm.
Stand watch in work, stand watch in play,
By night and noon, dark and day,
So be it.

If you wish, you can place a fifth candle for Spirit (preferably white) somewhere centrally located to make all five points of the pentagram. Even when the candles are not lit, this type of formation allows them to radiate an ambient protective energy.

Recovery (Mental, Physical, or Spiritual)

The energy of recovery has dimensions. It can aid someone when they're sick, bolster a sagging bottom line, and provide support when one's spirit has been dragged through the proverbial mud of a difficult situation. Recovery spells are like healing spells, except you're not only seeking reversal but also forward progress (or minimally a return to where you began, rather than ten paces behind that mark). You'll want to:

+ Time your spells for the waning moon (to
  decrease the power of the disease or problem),
  the waxing moon (to bring more positive
  energy to bear on the situation), Thursdays (for
  stamina), or Wednesdays (for ingenuity).

+ Add aromatics such as lilac, apple, and nutmeg (or those more specifically geared to your needs—such as rose for an emotional recovery from a relationship).

+ Use shoot-green candles (the color of healthy, new growth).

+ Include other components and symbols that you associate with recuperation and well-being, such as bandages, salve, soup, comfort foods, a red cross, and so on.

Spells

Let's begin with a candlepowered potion as an overall tonic (physical realm). For this blend, you'll want some apple juice and a hint of nutmeg. Light a green candle near your working area to support the magic. Warm the apple juice on the stove, stirring clockwise while saying:

> *Where sickness dwells, health impart,*
> *Positive magic stays, all negativity depart.*
> *Round the bow elixir true,*
> *By my will, my health renew.*

Pour this into a cup and move it to a spot where you can sit in the candle's renewing light. Sip slowly, letting the positive energy renew your body and spirit.

The symbolism of this next activity comes from the unique candleholder it uses. You'll need to find one of those thick, squishy balls that don't really hurt when they bounce off someone. Slice a little off the bottom so that it will sit flat on a surface, then make a round hole in the top—into which you'll eventually put a candle.

Next, carve your candle with the image of an eye or something else that you associate with mental functions.

Dab it with a bit of rosemary oil and secure it in your holder. Then, light the candle, saying:

> *Within my mind, renewal start.*
> *Within my will, strength impart.*
> *No matter the distractions, no matter the attack,*
> *My mind and spirit—like this flame—bounce back!*

(If you choose, you can repeat the incantation five times when you light the candle—the number of awareness—to empower it further.) Keep this candle in a safe place and light it any time you feel as if your mental edge is waning.

Having provided something for body and mind, let us turn to your spirit and soul, which need as much tending as the other two portions of self. Earlier, we talked about making a house candle to honor the spirit of a dwelling place. This activity is similar, but the spirit for whom you're creating the candle is your own.

Rather than using the traditional color and scent here, I suggest picking out your favorite color of wax and any aromatics you find uplifting. In the bottom of whatever mold you'll be using, place a little coconut butter (this hardens similarly to wax and has salve-like qualities). Because you're focusing on recovery, make the candle during the full moon or at the noon hour for blessings.

As you melt the wax and add your aromatics, focus on the wholeness of your spirit. Add a simple chant that you can repeat while working, such as:

> *By my will and the candle's flame,*
> *A renewal of spirit and soul I claim.*
> *Whenever this candle burns,*
> *Vitality to my spirit returns!*

Leave the candle in this setup and keep it in a special spot for when you're really lagging in spirit. This candle can also help empower various forms of magic in those moments where you feel your skills aren't quite *on*.

Relationships

We've spoken of love, friendship, and passion—but what of other types of interactions? There are the relationships we have with coworkers, pets, family, and community. Some are good, some not so good; however, inevitably, times arise when we need to strengthen or heal our ties. Unfortunately, circumstances and distance don't always make that easy. Spells and rituals give you a medium through which to answer the spiritual part of the equation while you continue your mundane efforts, no matter how far away the person (or persons) may be. So:

+ Time your spells for the month of July or Fridays (if the relationship is of a romantic nature), when the moon is in Pisces (to inspire fruitful friendships), or a waxing to full moon (to promote good feelings between people).

+ Add aromatics such as orange, rose, apple, basil, and lemon (all of which encourage warmth).

+ Use a candle whose color implies the type of relationship for which you're working magic. A business relationship might require a brown or green color to represent the Earth Element and prosperity, for example.

+ Include other components and symbols such as jade, knots, rings, cards, and forget-me-not type items.

Spells

Ever wish you could have just a glimmer of insight into a budding relationship? Candle scrying can help you predetermine a relationship's potential. For this first activity, you'll need at least fifteen minutes of quiet time, a candle whose color represents the potential partner, and a dark room. Please make sure there are no breezes around, as wind can wreak havoc on the results of a reading.

Begin by lighting the candle and getting comfortable somewhere nearby. If possible, place the candle's flame at eye level—that seems to work best. Think about a person you've recently gotten to know. Bring an image of them into your mind. Visualize the interactions you've had thus far, then focus on the question of what the most possible future holds for the two of you. (I say *possible* because your free will and actions from this moment forward can transform fate's web.)

Now, observe the flame's movements carefully. Try not to put your personal hopes and wishes into what you see. Simply observe. Here is a brief list of interpretive values:

Sparking

A potentially heated relationship, either through personalities that tend toward anger or a spark of passion. If the sparks fly to the right, it's a more positive omen.

Smoldering

Not much hope here. It will take plenty of effort to keep this relationship alive (especially if you want anything more than a short-term friendship or acquaintance).

Going Out

A truly negative sign. This relationship is going nowhere and may indeed be very bad for you. That said, if the candle burns for a few minutes before going out, it indicates you could have some fun times before the relationship ends.

Splitting in Two at the Top of the Wick
Twin flames with a solid body are a positive sign of two people with the potential to share one heart or goal.

Splitting Completely
An odd sign which either signals that someone intends to come between you and your companion, or that obstacles lie in your path.

Dancing or Burning Very Brightly
A positive sign of good energy between you two.

To help heal a relationship, come together with two candles (one candle per person) and two breakable items as representations of the issues that stand between you. Light your personal candles to signal your peaceful intentions. Speak openly and honestly about whatever is bothering you (direct this not only to each other but toward the breakable objects). Let those objects absorb your negativity completely.

When you're both done speaking your minds, put the two breakable items together on a piece of paper or cloth (to catch the shards) and break them together. These should be buried—or otherwise disposed of—to put the negativity away. Henceforth, these matters are dead and buried.

Finally, blow out the candles and wrap them in a white cloth (to protect the new peace you've created). Tie the bundle together with three knots—representing you, your companion, and the relationship—saying:

Peace has been reclaimed.
By our promise, animosity released.
From this moment onward, love will never cease.

Keep the candles somewhere safe and use them anytime you need to bring some gentle salve to your relationship.

Separation

Separation spells are not solely for relationships. They're also intended to help you transition between jobs, to a new residence, or from a split business partnership. The whole purpose of these rituals and spells is to provide closure and a positive new start:

+ Time your spells for winter, dusk, or the dark moon.

+ Add aromatics such as thyme (for courage), myrrh (for healing wounds), lotus (to break the ties between you), sage (for cleansing), and iris (for wisdom).

+ Use black candles (for endings), possibly coupled with green (for a healthy separation) or white ones (for pure intentions).

+ Include other components and symbols of separation, such as a partition, a knife, or scissors. Also, items that can be buried—to mark a figurative death.

Spells
For this first activity, you'll need to set up two candles with a long strand of thread in front of them. One candle represents you, and the other represents the person or situation from which you're separating. Mark each candle with an appropriate symbol before you begin.

Start with the candles sitting close together (the string in front should extend far beyond them on both sides).

At dusk on the first night, light them and separate the two by about an inch, saying:

Moving apart in body.

Blow out the candle (after focusing on the meaning of that phrase for a few minutes), turn, and walk away. Do not return to the candle until the second night.

On the second night, light the two candles and move them apart another inch, saying:

Moving apart in body, moving apart in mind.

Follow this with a brief meditation, blow out the candle, and walk away. The third night follows the same pattern using the incantation:

Moving apart in body,
moving apart in mind, moving apart in spirit.

This time, before you blow out the candles, cut the string before them in half. Keep the half that was near your personal candle wrapped around that candle and stow it away. The other half of the string and candle should be disposed of.

This next activity is for a couple that wishes to use candle symbolism to help with their separation. You'll need three candles in total: each person brings one, and the third represents the union. Each person should also bring symbols of the union that can be burned or destroyed for a clean ending.

This activity begins as the first one did, at sundown, with the central candle being lit. The couple should enter the room from opposite sides. Together, they'll light the individual candles from the union candle, saying:

I accept my light back without anger or blame.

Next, the two should blow out the union candle together, saying:

We release our bonds mutually, with all good wishes.

At this point, if there's anything else positive the individuals wish to convey to each other, they should.

Finally, any symbols of the relationship can be ritually burned or put away (possibly by a third party). From this point, the couple turns away, walking out again in opposite directions and not looking back. Symbolically, to look back is to hold on to the past. Learn from it, take the best, and leave the negativity firmly behind—where it belongs.

Service (Charity)

Life is no brief candle to me; it is a sort of splendid torch which I've got ahold of for the moment, and I want to make it burn as brightly as possible before handing it on to future generations.
—George Bernard Shaw

I know there have been many times when there was a need in our community that I wished myself and others could meet more effectively. That elder who's been stuck on the road for a long time may need some service. The family whose main breadwinner has been unemployed for an extended period may need a little unobtrusive charity. In either case, our intervention is important to keeping our community whole. This flavor of Candle Magic is designed to encourage a generous heart and spirit where they're most needed. To use it:

✦ Time your spells as needed. Sunlight
   accents more mental-physical service, while
   moonlight accents spiritual service.

✦ Add aromatics such as peach (for wisdom), marigold
   (for sensitivity and awareness), ginger (for energy),
   lavender (for harmony), and lily (for happiness).

✦ Use a candle whose color represents the individual
   or group toward whom you're directing the magic.

✦ Include other components and symbols, such as a
   serving tray or open hands (palms up). A good stone
   for spiritual service is sugilite, while tiger's eye helps
   the body, and fluorite assists the mind and skills.

Spells

This first spell is intended to open a community's heart to
someone (or to a group) who has a specific need. It is carefully
contrived so as not to overstep free will but rather to illuminate
the area of need.

Begin with a candle into which you've carved the name
of the person or group in need. Place this on an altar—or
in another special spot—and surround it with marigold
petals, saying:

> *Flowers of kindness surround you,*
> *Petals of gentle charity reach out to you,*
> *Budding consideration opens to you,*
> *Let every need be seen and met.*
> *So mote it be.*

Light this candle once a day at dawn (perhaps while you
get ready for work) and repeat the incantation or meditate on

the person or group toward whom this energy is directed. This is also a good time to do a little networking on their behalf (write emails, call, send a letter or two describing the need and how those you're contacting can help).

When the need passes, release the marigold petals to the Four Winds to bless the Earth and others in need whose paths they cross.

This next activity allows you to direct spiritually supportive energy to a leader, elder, or teacher who needs a boost. (Technically, you can use the first candle spell given here to accomplish this simply by changing the wording. However, I want to provide you with an alternative format with which to work.)

If possible, have a picture of the person on hand (or something from them, such as a letter). Place a rainbow assortment of candles around this item (so that they can receive whatever type of energy they most need). Light these daily for a few minutes and say a brief prayer aimed toward that individual. Visualize them, extending the energy of the flames and your words outward.

Save the remaining wax from those candles and remelt them during a full moon, adding some symbolic aromatics. Send this to the person if possible, or simply reuse the candle to keep the positive energy going.

Sleep (Rest)

Having lived in the city with three children, I'm aware of the many things that can disrupt a person's sleep. I also live with an insomniac who goes through cycles of very uneven sleep patterns. This life experience brought about some personal ponderings about sleep and, in turn, the spell-related insights that follow:

✦ Time your spells for bedtime to get the best results.

✦ Add calming aromatics such as
   chamomile, lavender, and mint.

✦ Use a purple candle (for a dreamy sleep),
   a white candle (for uninterrupted sleep),
   or a blue candle (for overall calm).

✦ Include other components and symbols such as
   coral (specifically used for helping children sleep)
   or moonstone (better for adults). Also include
   anything associated with sleep, such as your pillow,
   favorite blanket, sheep (for counting), and so on.

Spells

This first activity begins with a warm lavender tea and a candle dressed with lavender oil. Take about 1/8 of a cup of lavender and steep it in a cup of water (just the petals). While that steeps, dress and light the candle. Breathe deeply. Lavender has a very relaxing quality. Hold the cup in both hands and empower the beverage by saying:

> *Even as I drink this deep,*
> *bring to me a night of sleep.*

Quaff the potion, blow out the candle, and let yourself float gently on the aroma of lavender off to sleep.

By the way, if you have some extra lavender flower, it's often beneficial to put a bundle of it (sachet-sized) under your pillow to keep the effect going all night.

For this next activity, you'll need about eight light blue tapers and one other candle that represents the situation or person in need of tranquility. Each night, around the time when most people are starting to relax, surround that central candle with the blue ones and light them while reciting calming words. For example, if you're working magic to help with your own sleeping patterns, say:

> *Stillness, calm, quiet ensure...*
> *bring to me a sleep that's pure.*

To bring rest to a group that seems to be struggling, try:

> *Goddess, hear my sincere behest,*
> *Bring to (name) some calm and rest!*

Leave the candles to burn for a while, and if possible, remain there to direct the energy. Then, blow them out.

Continue this routine for as long as necessary to achieve results.

This last sleep and dream charm involves a little bit of sewing. For it, you'll need a swatch of some nice fabric or a lace doily, a moonstone crystal bead, a feather, some thread, and, of course, a nice dark blue candle! During the waxing to full moon, decoratively attach the crystal and feather to the doily or fabric—near its edge somewhere. As you sew these in place, repeat this incantation five times:

> *On night's wings, sweet dreams my magic brings;*
> *As moonstone shines, restful sleep will be mine!*

Place the sewn doily and fabric swatch on a surface near your bed. Put the dark blue candle atop this doily and light it every night before sleeping, repeating the incantation. Take a few moments to meditate and relax before the candle, then blow it out and enjoy a peaceful night's sleep.

(Sidenote: because this activity tends to bring sweet dreams, too, you may want to keep a pen and paper near your bed!)

Travel

Travel spells focus on manifesting smooth, worry-free excursions. The next time you're going on a family outing, taking a vacation, or have another adventure planned, enact travel-oriented candlelight spells *first* so that you have the most fun possible. To do so:

+ Time your spells for just prior to your journey—or during the planning process.

+ Add protective aromatics such as violet, clove, fennel, lilac, coconut, and sage.

+ Use a white candle (for protection) or a yellow one (for movement).

+ Include other components and symbols such as tin or turquoise (carried as amulets), maps and tour books, miniature vehicles, and corks with coins (for sea travel).

Spells
Make yourself a portable travel amulet! Begin with a white candle and a yellow candle into which you've carved images of the type(s) of transportation you'll be using (you should make each carving specific). If you're able to find a toy model to use for this charm, all the better—but a suitable crystal will do, along with some protective aromatics. Melt your candles in a non-aluminum pot over a low flame. Stir counterclockwise, saying:

> *From here to there, and there to here,*
> *Have no worries, have no fears;*
> *Home or away, away or home,*
> *In my (type of transportation), I'll safely roam.*

Fill in the blank with your type(s) of transportation (plane, car, bike, motorcycle, and so on).

When the wax is completely melted, add your aromatic. Let this cool until you can handle it easily. Shape the semi-warm wax around the crystal (or toy token) that represents your mode of travel, surrounding it with protective energy. Keep this on hand as you travel. (Sidenote: if you live in a hot environment, you may wish to wrap this bundle yet again with aluminum foil, wax, paper, or another protective wrap to keep it from melting and making a mess.)

Save a few drops of wax from your first activity and mark your home on a map with it. Also mark the location where you're traveling with the safety-charged wax. Next, take a toy car, plane, bus, or train and follow the route you'll be taking (if flying, be as approximate as possible). Move the toy slowly and purposefully from home to the destination, saying:

> *Adventure waits, I call on the Fates;*
> *Protect my path, guide the way;*
> *Keep all dangers and delays at bay!*

Keep repeating this little chant while you move the vehicle. Afterward, you can take both the map and the toy with you as amulets.

In Victorian times, people carried mint to encourage safe voyages. Blending this idea with Candle Magic isn't difficult. For this next spell, you'll need a grey candle that's been dressed with mint oil, as well as a mint leaf. Light the candle, visualizing the trip ahead (even if it's going to the office) and saying:

Like the light of this candle surrounds,
Safety and protection abounds.
Even when the flame ceases to shine,
The magic within this leaf binds.
(Drip some wax on the mint leaf.)
As the point between dark and day,
This amulet to protect me,
Keep all dangers at bay.

Tuck the mint leaf into your purse, wallet, or briefcase, and head out. Keep in mind: it's not necessary to do this every morning. You can just light the candle while you prepare for work and blow it out as you walk out the door. If the mint leaf becomes brittle and cracks, however, you should prepare a new one.

Transformation

We must view young people not as empty bottles
to be filled, but as candles to be lit.
—Robert H. Shaffer

Life is change. And these days, it seems like changes come at warp speeds, often leaving us breathless. We have to integrate plenty of external and internal transformations daily—it certainly won't hurt to use a little candlepower to assist in that process. Transformation spells can help you process a change, get changes moving in the right direction, and adjust to unwanted changes. To use them:

+ Time your spells for midnight, dawn, or dusk (when time itself is transforming along with the light). New Year's Eve is also a good time.

+ Add aromatics such as nutmeg (determination), orange (tenacity and luck), and balm (manifestation).

+ Use any color of candle you prefer. The melting of the wax is, in itself, a strong symbol of change. However, you can choose the candle's color so it correlates to the area of your life where transformation is most needed.

+ Include other components and symbols that have various states. For example, water can become steam or ice, tides shift and change, and crackers crumble. Eggs can be broken for breakfast or hatched. Caterpillars become butterflies. Also consider tools that help us transform things from one state to another (such as a blender or food processor, which makes things liquid).

Spells

For this first activity, begin with a piece of soft clay, a carefully preserved eggshell filled with dirt, a flowering seed, and a birthday candle (which is placed within the eggshell and held in place by the dirt). Make a thumbprint impression in the clay that can hold the eggshell upright for the duration of the spell.

Wait until dawn (for a positive change), then light the candle and say:

As dawn gives way today…light the way, light the way.
As my path is rearranged, help me accept gentle change.

Blow out the candle as you would for any wish and set it aside. Take the eggshell out to some good soil—nearby, so you can tend to it—and plant it in the ground. By the time the seed begins to sprout, your transitions should be rolling along smoothly.

I have frequently found butterfly-shaped candles at dollar stores and gift shops. These are ideal for transformation magic. Even if you can't find one, you can carve the image of a butterfly onto a candle of your choice. Use this as the starting point for a candlelight visualization.

As you look into the flame, imagine that glow getting larger and larger—surrounding you like a cocoon. It's warm and comforting. You know you're wholly safe. Within this energy shell, you can make whatever shifts in awareness or thinking that you most need. Take your time. Breathe deeply. Don't rush this process.

As you're working through those items, imagine yourself growing wings like the butterfly you carved on the candle. The light around you gathers and shapes them; these are wings of power and light and life! By the end of the visualization, the energy that surrounded you at first will have wholly poured itself into your spiritual wings so that you can lift yourself above the circumstances and find success.

This last activity takes place at a beach at sunset. The visual effect of this location is really beautiful, but if you can't get to a beach, you can use a box of sand, a candle, and any water source instead. Wait for the sun to glow warmly on the horizon's edge. Light your candle, using the beach to hold it upright. Speak your needs and wishes into the water.

Next, find a spot nearby to sit, watch, and wait. Let yourself be filled by the ever-moving waters that shift with ease. Become as the flow that fills any shape. If possible, stay until the water extinguishes the candle, and gather up a little sand and wax to keep in a pouch as a charm that keeps the magic moving with you.

Truth

The truth can be a very subjective thing, but there are times when you need harsh objectivity and a reality check. When you sense that you may not be getting the whole picture—or that something is too good to be true—shine a light on it with Candle Magic. To do so:

+ Time your spells for when the stars are shining or when the moon is full.

+ Add aromatics such as peach (insight), saffron (wisdom), rose (foresight), and mint (clarity and awareness).

+ Use a white candle.

+ Include other components and symbols, such as bloodstone and malachite (discernment), the Earth (people used to vow honesty with one hand on the ground), binoculars (or anything that magnifies), a mirror (for self-truth), and owls (the messengers of truth).

Spells

Enact this spell five hours before you go on a fact-finding mission. Begin with five white candles. Come the first hour, light the first candle, saying:

> *One: the light of truth to savor,*
> *And from it, I shall not waiver.*

Come the second hour, light the second candle from the first, saying:

> *One: the light of truth to savor,*
> *And from it, I shall not waiver.*
> *Two: the glow of honest words,*
> *Spirit, listen—let my prayer be heard.*

Come the third hour, light the third candle from the first and second, saying:

> *One: the light of truth to savor,*
> *And from it, I shall not waiver.*
> *Two: the glow of honest words,*
> *Spirit, listen—let my prayer be heard.*
> *Three: the flame of sincerity,*
> *Through all lies, let my eyes see.*

The fourth and fifth hours follow the same pattern with these additional verses:

> *Four: the glimmer of something hidden or sealed,*
> *By this magic, let all be revealed.*
> *Five: the spark of good intent,*
> *From will to world, my spell is sent.*

If you wish, you can take some wax drippings with you from all five candles as a truth talisman.

For this last spell, go to a dusty surface with a candle and a soft cloth. Set the candle down, light it, then rub the surface counterclockwise, saying:

> *Uncertainty erase, the truth to face,*
> *Reality shine, by this spell, the truth will be mine.*

(To clarify: you're not really trying to clean the surface here, but rather create a swirling pattern in the dust.) Now stop and scry the surface using the candle's reflection on the surface. Think of the situation in which you feel you're not getting the whole truth. Watch for images or specific movements to appear in the swirls. Movement upward and to the right of the image means *yes,* you're not getting all the information you need. Movement downward or left means *no;* everything is as it seems. Clockwise inward-moving spirals mean you're getting closer to the truth, while outward counterclockwise ones mean that you're looking in the wrong direction.

Unconscious Mind

Throughout his life's work, psychiatrist and author Carl Jung talked about the collective unconscious among humans—the well of information and knowledge to which we all have access. This theory explains why various people all get the same idea even when separated by miles, cultural differences, and even time. We cannot begin to tap this well if we haven't first gotten to know our own subconscious and superconsciousness. In spiritual traditions, it's important to remain aware that there is a lot going on, that the conscious mind doesn't always register. In effect, we file it into the subconscious to be retrieved in dreams, visions, and those periodic light-bulb moments when we say, "Ah-*ha!*" This type of Candle Magic is designed to help you get back in touch with the inner worlds where mind and spirit interact more readily. To use it:

+ Time your spells for when the moon is waxing to full or Mondays (the moon's day).

+ Add lunar and psychic aromatics such as bay leaves, honeysuckle, lemongrass, marigold, mint, rose, vanilla, and thyme.

182

✦ Use silver or white candles to represent the moon.

✦ Include other components and symbols of the higher self and spiritual pursuits such as silver, moonstone, cat's eye, rowan, or willow wood.

Spells

Awakening your latent skills and insights takes practice. Thankfully, candles are inexpensive tools with which to practice. Specifically, you can learn to hone your intuitive self by making wax patterns on paper or water.

Begin by drawing an eye on a piece of paper. Place this paper on a tabletop and think of a simple question. Next, take a yellow candle that is lit and hold it over the paper, saying:

> *Knowledge be clear by candlelight;*
> *Grant to me the gift of sight!*

Put the candle aside and look at the paper, especially around the eye. Let your vision blur slightly, and then make note of any impressions you get. Such patterns or pictures can be looked up in a dream dictionary or other divinatory correspondence list. The idea here is to hone your ability—to tap into the unconscious mind by using it more often.

If you decide you'd like to try the water approach instead, place a clear bowl of water on top of the drawing of the eye or, perhaps, a window (to open the inner windows of the Self). Then, simply drip the wax (more than one color if you wish) into the water and look for the emerging patterns. This time, try an incantation while you're looking at the surface, like:

> *From my spirit, nothing is sealed;*
> *In this wax, insights revealed!*

Another good way to empower the unconscious and intuitive self is through this meditation. Go outside on a night when you can see the moon clearly. Take your candle with you (anointed with an aromatic of your choice). Get comfortable and look at the candle as you begin to breathe deeply and relax. Make sure you can visualize the candle's flame clearly in your mind before you close your eyes.

The main chakras governing the unconscious or superconscious mind are those of the heart, third eye, and crown. Your heart center is located in the middle of your chest; the third eye, between your eyes on your forehead; and the crown is where a baby's soft spot would be in an adult. Begin at the heart center, visualizing the flame of your candle right in front of it. Let the light be wholly absorbed by that region (you'll feel warm or tingly).

Next, move the flame in front of your third eye chakra. See the warm flames swirling clockwise inward, overflowing it with energy. Finally, move the flame to your crown chakra and let the energy sprinkle down over you like rain. Continue as long as you wish, and write notes about your experience afterward.

Victory (Success)

The ego is an important element of human awareness. While none of us wants it running amok, having self-confidence and a sense of true success in specific areas of our lives is healthy and necessary. Nonetheless, there are times when our daily reality hands us proverbial lemons. When you want your resulting lemonade to be all the sweeter and that victory to finally arrive after all your hard work, bring some magic into the equation for just the right push. To do so:

+ Time your spells for dawn or spring (when light overcomes darkness). Also, the blue moon is a good time (especially if you need a figurative miracle).

+ Add successful aromatics such as lemon, cinnamon, ginger, and pine.

+ Use gold or silver candles (gold for larger successes). Alternatively, vibrant yellow or orange will work.

+ Include other components and symbols that represent victory. For example, blue ribbons imply winning a competition. Other fortunate components include agates, hematite, amber, bloodstone, and any items bearing solar imagery.

Spells

This first spell is delightfully simple. Right before you go into a situation where you need a real victory, take out a candle and dab it with a bit of lemon essence. If possible, place this candle where it can safely burn unattended while you're going about the necessary task(s). Light the candle, saying:

> *As the candle burns brighter,*
> *Bring the success desired.*

Repeat the incantation eight times to build strong foundations, then move forward with confidence.

For this next activity, we're going to begin by using the symbolic value of a blue ribbon braided with a gold one (solar blessings) and a golden candle. Light the golden candle so that it shines while you're working. Take two blue ribbons to one central gold, and as you braid them, recite this little verse repeatedly until you're done:

> *Ribbons of blue, the victory's mine.*
> *Ribbon of gold, my skills, how they shine.*
> *Magic within, braided and bound,*
> *A victory, sure, will soon come round!*

Drop a bit of wax on the ribbon's ends so that they don't fray, and carry this token as a success charm. You can now light the candle and repeat the incantation to further support the charm or even use it to burn paper images of things you feel are holding you back from a clean victory.

Virtue (Honor)

The importance of the words *honor, respect,* and *gratitude* has already been stressed. Honor and virtue are not outmoded values for the true spiritual seeker. When one honors something, they are much less likely to abuse it (and, in fact, are more likely to appreciate it all the more). Virtue is our guiding light in how to act and react at every moment of every day. Now, as lofty as that sounds, there are days when I want to toss all my ideals out the window because of a perceived injustice or harm. While there may be times to take up arms and fight, these spells are intended for those moments when you need to reconnect with your own sense of right and wrong—and stand by it without fail. So:

+ Time your spells for the daylight hours
  (honor never hides in the shadows).

+ Add aromatics such as thyme (courage), nutmeg
  (for holding firm to a belief), cedar
  (protection), and marigold (justice).

+ Use a white candle for pure motivation
  and thoughtful action.

+ Include other components and symbols that
  represent these qualities to you (I use the image of a
  knight or his lady's favor as one example). Also, any
  white piece of clothing can imply virtue (purity).

Spells

When you're not sure what the best, most honorable decision is, this is a nice, candlelit prayer that you can say every morning and evening until the choice becomes clear. Start by lighting the candle of your choice, then say:

> *Light of spirit, light of truth,*
> *Illuminate the way between right and wrong,*
> *Let my path be sure, my will be strong,*
> *Show me where my efforts belong.*
> *Spirit of truth, Spirit of light,*
> *Help me make the choice that's right!*

This is a little chant that can go with you anywhere. (Also: pay particular attention to any dreams you have during the period you're enacting this spell, as they may reveal your best course of action.)

When you face a situation where there's the temptation to do something you know is wrong, bring to your mind's eye the image of a white candle to provide energy and to light your way in the murky waters that surround. Then, silently or out loud, say:

> *The effect of respect*
> *Is an attitude of gratitude!*
> *Honor, goodness, and trust*
> *In my actions are a must!*

Continue to repeat this to yourself until you find that knee-jerk reaction calming; that way, you can walk away with your karma intact.

Weather

As the old saying goes, "if you want the weather to change, wait five minutes." Or, you could cast a spell! I share weather-oriented spells with a warning. Bear in mind that you're playing with the patterns of an entire world. By trying to play push-me, pull-you with a stormfront, you could be robbing an area of much-needed water (as an example). So, think carefully about what you need, when you need it, and why. To provide a personal illustration, I was performing an outdoor wedding for a dear friend, and a serious storm was prevailing. Rather than try to stop it, I asked for a one-hour holding pattern in my magic. It worked perfectly (but I got only sixty minutes—not one second more)! This met my need without completely disrupting Mother Nature.

Because different types of weather require different candle colors and aromatics, refer to the following section (set up according to the weather desired):

Rain

When you want to bring rain, sprinkle damp heather around a lit candle (so that it appears to be raining), then blow it out (water douses fire). Add an incantation to this process that indicates the amount of rain desired—and for how long— to achieve the best results. If you want to make a portable rain charm, use the same candle, gather up a bit of heather, and put it in a pouch with a quartz crystal and a few drops of wax. Release all but the candle to a living water source to invoke rain.

Sun

To clear away the clouds in the sky, begin by lighting a yellow or gold candle to honor the sun. Then, take a piece of kelp (or any Water-oriented stone) and bury it in sand or dirt (this also quells wind). To that foundation, you can certainly add a chant: for example, the childhood rhyme of "rain, rain, go away" works as a perfectly viable invocation.

Snow or Mist

Living in Western New York, it's hard to imagine anyone *wanting* snow, but should this be a desire, light a white candle and take it—along with a piece of jade—to a source of living water. Toss the stone in the water. Stay in that location with the candle held high (lighting the way for weather spirits) and add an invocation should you wish.

Wind

To raise a wind, light a yellow candle (this honors the Air Element). Then toss either some saffron or broom toward the East with a simple invocation such as:

Let the winds begin!

Alternatively, you can make a wind rope, inspired by Arab customs, by binding a piece of broom or saffron to a rope with a drop of yellow wax. Make three knots this way. Undo one knot when you want a light breeze, two for a fuller-forced wind. Do not release the third; that is considered greedy.

Wisdom

> *To light one candle to God and another to the Devil*
> *is the principle of wisdom.*
> —Jose Bergamin

Ah, my kingdom to have been wiser when much younger. There are so many situations that challenge our sagacity: making decisions in child-rearing, choosing a path, dealing with coworkers, or even balancing a budget. All of these moments provide an opportunity to put the symbolism of candles to work yet again:

+ Time your spells according to the area of your life in which you need wisdom. For example, wisdom on your spiritual path is best accomplished by working with a full moon, whereas conscious wisdom for daily tasks is more solar in nature.

+ Add aromatics such as iris, peach, and sage, all of which support this goal.

+ Use purple candles (especially for spiritual wisdom).

+ Include other sagacious components and symbols, such as an owl. Among stones, we find jade (especially for wisdom in relationships), sodalite, and sugilite. Edible items include almonds, peaches, and olives.

Spells

Use this potion for balanced wisdom. Begin with a dark purple candle lit in the kitchen while you're working. When you ignite the candle, say:

> *Wisdom's light shine, within and without,*
> *Conscious wisdom be mine!*

Next, grab some peach juice (you can find this type of blend in most frozen food sections or natural food co-ops; if you can't access it, a fresh peach works effectively too). Leave it adjacent to the candle in a sunny window of the kitchen for about five minutes to absorb the light. Then, blow out the candle and put the glass of juice away until evening.

When the moon rises, repeat the procedure, but alter the incantation to:

> *Wisdom's light shine within and without,*
> *Intuitive wisdom, be mine!*

Again, leave these two items in the moonlight for a few minutes, then drink the juice to internalize the energy.

To bring wisdom into your profession, find two nice candleholders, a purple candle, and one candle that represents your work. Carve the purple candle with an image of an eye (for example, the Eye of Ra) for insight. Carve the other candle with an image of your profession (for example, if you're a writer, carve a quill or pen).

On the three nights of the full moon, enact this spell. Place the two candles across from each other on a table or altar. Each night, as the moon rises, light the business candle from the wisdom candle, saying:

> *Like this candle's light;*
> *My wisdom shines bright!*

Afterward, move the candles slightly closer together and let them burn for forty minutes (four being an Earth-oriented number). Proceed on the second and third nights as with the first—but by the third night, the candles should be sitting side by side. When the forty minutes are over, blow out the candles and bind them together. If possible, keep these at your place of work or store them with symbols of your problem.

Wishes

Children and adults from all walks of life practice wishing. It is one of the most user-friendly forms of will-driven magic. And considering how at least one of those forms of wishing comes in blowing out birthday candles, why not take the whole concept further? If the lighting of a candle indicates our intention, then its flame and smoke can send our wishes out to the Universe. To make a candlelit wish:

+ Time your spells for when the stars are shining or when the moon is full.

+ Add aromatics typically associated with wishing, such as sage, sandalwood, and violet.

+ Use a candle whose color represents the area of your life at which the wish is directed.

+ Include other components and symbols on which people wish, such as coins, birthday candles, and four-leaf clovers.

Spells

This first wish spell is simple and only requires that you have a bay leaf and a candle of a suitable color for your goal. Write a word on the bay leaf that describes your wish. Light this in the flame of your candle, saying:

> *By the candlelight, wish take to flight;*
> *Burned by the fire, my wishes go higher;*
> *In the smoke, it's free, so mote it be!*

(Note: you will want to have a small fireproof container nearby that you can put the bay leaf in to burn up completely.) Continue chanting while it burns, then release the ashes to the Four Winds, trusting the energy to manifest.

This next activity is a fun adaptation of the French tradition of floating candles with wishes. You can enact it on a pool or in the stream of a hose, but rivers, lakes, or oceans (living water sources) seem to work better. You'll need a child's toy boat (preferably a wooden one so that it's biodegradable). Alternatively, you can make a float for your candle by binding popsicle sticks together, raft-style, or by using a floating candle.

On top of this foundation, put a small votive candle dabbed with an oil corresponding to your goal. Light the candle, then gently launch the ship on the chosen water, saying:

> *By will and wish, by wish and will,*
> *The light of this candle shall fulfill;*
> *As it floats out of sight,*
> *I extend my wish with all my might;*
> *The light of hope on currents strong,*
> *Take my wish where it belongs.*

Continue reciting this rhyme until you can no longer see the candle.

AFTERWORD

This exploration of Candle Magic has been fun and challenging for me. There were times while I was writing when I thought, *What else can I possibly do with a candle?* As you can see, candles certainly withstood that creative dare with a unique flare—and truly surprised me. They are an incredibly flexible tool that no Witch's kit is complete without.

I hope you find these ideas helpful, that they inspire more of your own, and that, akin to a candle in the dark, you shine this knowledge and magic into the world. With that thought, I leave you these wonderful words:

> *Sound when stretched is music.*
> *Movement when stretched is dance.*
> *Mind when stretched is meditation.*
> *Life, when stretched is celebration.*

— Sri Sri Ravi Shankar, *Celebrating Silence*

APPENDIX A:
HISTORICAL TIDBITS, FOLKS BELIEFS, AND HELPFUL HINTS

Historical Tidbits

+ History indicates that the Egyptians were perhaps the first people to make and use candles.

+ Candles are mentioned in biblical writings as early as the tenth century BCE.

+ By canon law, candles used in certain rituals of the Roman Catholic Church must have a composition of at least 51% beeswax. The remainder may be a vegetable or a mineral wax but not tallow.

+ Greeks and Romans were the first to add wicks to the candle's construction.

+ Candles have been made out of a multitude of base materials, including tallow, insect wax, seed wax, bayberry, spermaceti, palm leaves, candlefish, paraffin, and Cerio tree wax.

+ The simplest (and smelliest) candles, rushlights, were made by dipping rushes in leftover kitchen fat.

+ The first dipped candles, made with beeswax, originated in the 1200s, followed by molded candles in the 1400s, and then by automated candle-making machines in the 1800s.

✦ The English-owned Tallow Chandlers' Company was incorporated in 1462, and they regulated trade in candles made from animal fats.

✦ Some of the more advanced candlemakers would bleach their candles by hanging them outside for as long as eight to ten days.

✦ American pioneer homes achieved fancy striped effects by using the red juice of pokeberries, wild nettles for green, alder bark for yellow, and other natural dyestuffs.

✦ In 1834, inventor Joseph Morgan introduced a machine that allowed for the continuous production of molded candles through the use of a cylinder, which itself featured a movable piston that ejected candles as they solidified.

✦ Also in the nineteenth century, changes took place in the design of the candlewicks. Instead of being made by simply twisting strands of cotton, wicks were now plaited tightly. As a result, the burned portion curled over and was consumed rather than falling messily into the melting wax.

✦ The term *candlepower* is based on a measurement of the light produced by a pure spermaceti candle weighing 1/6 of a pound, burning at a rate of 120 grams per hour.

✦ America's first contribution to candle-making was when they discovered that boiling the grayish-

green berries of bayberry bushes produced a
sweet-smelling wax that burned cleanly.

+ The first standard candles were made from
spermaceti wax. Spermaceti was obtained
through a crystallization process, and it did
not elicit a repugnant odor when burned.
Furthermore, spermaceti wax was found to
be harder than both tallow and beeswax.

Folk Beliefs

+ The gift of a candle to newlyweds ensures
them of providence and fertility.

+ Lighting a candle with your right hand brings luck.

+ Letting candles burn out naturally—especially
on special occasions—improves good fortune.

+ To avoid problems, never light more
than two candles from one match.

+ Bayberry candles presented on New
Year's bring health and money.

+ A candle that goes out without explanation is either a
bad omen or indicates the presence of a restless ghost.

+ A candle that refuses to light portends
a storm on the horizon (which can be
real or figurative, like an emotion).

✦ Candle flames that shape themselves into the form of a ring predict a forthcoming marriage in the household.

✦ A burning candle placed inside a hollowed-out pumpkin or jack-o'-lantern on Samhain works to keep evil spirits and demons at bay.

✦ For good luck, burn black and orange candles on Halloween, then gaze into them to see the future.

✦ If a candle falls and breaks in two, double trouble will come to you.

✦ To dream of a white candle portends true love.

✦ Seeing two candles in a dream is a sign of a forthcoming marriage proposal.

✦ A red candle in a dream symbolizes passion and sexual desire.

✦ To dream of five candles predicts love and marriage.

✦ To dream of a candle set firmly in a holder is an omen of a happy and prosperous future.

✦ Dreaming of a candleholder without a candle in it foretells sorrow.

✦ Always light candles at moments of birth, marriage, and death. This keeps malevolent spirits away.

+ Light a brown candle at Candlemas
  for protection against ghosts.

+ In Sicily, fishermen burn ornate candles for
  their patron saint to obtain blessings.

+ A pink candle burned on Valentine's
  Day inspires love and devotion.

+ A burning candle placed in a window will ensure
  the safe return of a lover traveling abroad.

+ To test the fidelity of a lover, light a candle
  outdoors near their house. If the flame burns
  towards you, your lover is faithful.

+ To reclaim the affections of a lost lover, thrust
  two pins or needles through the wick of a
  burning candle as you say their name.

+ Light a green candle on a night of
  the new moon for prosperity.

+ A candle lit from the hearth fire prevents wealth.

Helpful Hints

+ Remove candle wax from fabric by laying
  newspaper over it, placing a warm iron (set on
  low) over top, and rubbing it gently. Repeat,
  allowing the paper to absorb the melted wax.

+ To dispose of unwanted wax, pour the liquid
  into a milk carton for garbage disposal.

✦ Soft cloths can remove minor bits of dirt or scratches from stored candles.

✦ Chilling candles—or washing them in cold water first—helps them burn evenly and last longer (freezing also retains the aroma).

✦ If a candle loses its aroma, just dab it with some essential oil.

✦ Wrap scented candles and store them separately from others to keep the aromas from mixing.

✦ Trim candle wicks to 1/4 of an inch to avoid soot marks on the ceiling of a room.

✦ Use a piece of aluminum foil in the bottom of a candleholder to help keep a wobbly candle steady.

✦ When the sides of a pillar candle get too high and extinguish the wick, simply trim back the top of the candle and save those remnants for the making of another taper!

✦ When you are short on time and still want to do a candle spell, use a birthday candle! The budget-minded Witch can go to dollar stores to get inexpensive candles, holders, and even aromatic oils.

✦ If possible, get yourself the "aim and flame" type of lighter for Candle Magic. This will keep you from burning your fingers, especially on hard-to-reach wicks.

APPENDIX B:
USEFUL CORRESPONDENCES

Colors

If you wish to infuse your homemade candles with natural colorings, keep in mind that the magical correspondence of the plants used will add to the candles' energy. Rose coloring comes from bloodroot (protection, love), a gold color can be obtained from the oxeye daisy (Fire and solar energy), tansy leaves (health) yield a green hue, myrrh (spirituality, well-being) provides orange tinting, and marigold (dreams, psychicism) makes yellow.

The following list describes the relationship between candle colors and astrological signs, as well as their combined attributes:

Black
Virgo, Libra, Capricorn
Banishing, quiet, restfulness, grief, acceptance, parting. Use on Saturdays with jet or obsidian.

Blue
Aquarius, Gemini, Libra, Pisces, Virgo
Peace, comprehension, patience, noble ideals, opportunity, trust, truth, justice. Use on Thursdays with lapis or turquoise.

Brown
Capricorn, Scorpio, Cancer
Grounding, Earth energies, fate, resolution, hearth and home, balance, foundations, acceptance. Use on Saturdays with brown agate or tiger's eye.

Gold
Leo, Virgo, Sagittarius
Solar Magic, God-oriented, victory, overcoming, improved outlooks, wealth, honor, longevity, ambition. Use on Sundays with yellow-colored crystals.

Grey
Any sign
Neutrality, invisibility, compromise. Use any day with gray banded agate.

Green
Aquarius, Pisces, Cancer, Virgo
Growth, health, money, luck, sympathy, Earth Magic, tonic qualities. Use on Fridays with jade moss agate.

Orange
Sagittarius
The harvest, encouragement, joy, motivation, fertility, self-confidence, abundance. Use on Sundays with crystals, such as carnelian.

Pink
Taurus, Aries
Friendship, honor, goodness, peace, romance, emotional healing, sleep, forgiveness. Use on Fridays with rose quartz.

Purple
Aquarius, Pisces, Libra
Spirituality, wisdom, psychism, dream work, happiness, comprehension, spiritual healing. Use on Thursdays with amethyst or sugilite.

Red
Taurus, Gemini, Leo, Aries, Scorpio
Power, passion, health, courage, Fire Element, energy, tenacity, mental keenness, strength, overcoming. Use on Tuesdays with red crystals such as jasper.

Silver
Cancer
Moon Magic, Goddess-oriented, divination, astral work, insight. Use on Mondays with white-colored stones.

White
Pisces, Aries
Cleansing, truth, purity, enthusiasm, healing, Goddess energy, focus, protection, consecration, connecting with spirit guides, beginnings. Use on Mondays in combination with clear quartz or white stones.

Yellow
Taurus, Leo, Sagittarius, Gemini
Communication, certainty, Air Element, business improvements, improved memory and concentration, the conscious mind. Use on Wednesdays with citrine.

(Note: various sources disagree on the astrological associations of colors, and I've only included the most common ones out there—so please, trust your instincts!)

Numbers

Numbers can be carved into candles. Alternatively, an incantation can be repeated a supportive number of times, or a candle and components left to charge for a symbolic number of hours or minutes.

1. Personal Magic, completion, solar energy.
2. United effort, cooperation, partnership.
3. The body-mind-spirit trinity, fortitude.
4. Earth, cycles, foundations, money matters.
5. Alertness, awakenings, the Elements in balance.
6. Tenacity, completion, protection.
7. Water, the moon, diversity, perspective.
8. Leadership, changes, logical mind, concrete reality.
9. Giving to receive, service, the mysteries.
10. Solar and God energies.

Stones

Use stones in, on, or near your candles to support the magic and so that you have a portable talisman after working to keep the energies close at hand.

Agate
Protection, Gardening Magic, Earth energies.

Amber
Health and storing energy.

Amethyst
Self-control, truth, psychism.

Bloodstone
Stress relief, restoring emotional balance.

Carnelian
Overall tonic qualities, blessings, hope, honesty.

Coral
Water energies, protection of children, improved perspectives.

Fluorite
Effective application of one's skills, confidence.

Jade
Love, protecting relationships.

Jasper
Weather working.

Lapis
Spirituality and meditation.

Malachite
Precognition.

Moonstone
Lunar energy, nurturing, awareness, luck.

Quartz
Good all-purpose stone (clear quartz).

Rose Quartz
Self-love, gentle feelings, friendship.

Tourmaline
Creativity, banishing fear, inner peace.

Turquoise
Safe travel, communication.

Shapes and Images

Carve shapes and images into the candles or incorporate them into amulets, charms, or talismans (preferably in a wax base).

Almond Shape
Spiritual energy (feminine).

Anchor
Stability.

Ankh
Health and longevity.

Arrow
Guiding energy, accomplishment.

Circle
The moon or sun, cycles, safety.

Crescent Moon
Protection from evil.

Cross (or X)
Elemental Balance, reaching goals successfully.

Dollar Sign
Prosperity Magic.

Eye
Understanding, vision, comprehension.

Feather
Air Element.

Hexagram
The connection between the spiritual and temporal.

Hourglass
Time's movement.

Key
Opening, opportunity, unlocking a mystery.

Knot
Binding or unbinding energy.

Line
Singularity, the Path.

Runes
This depends on the rune (each of which has its own value), but all are easily carved.

Shield
Bravery, safety, agility.

Smile
Happiness.

Spiral
Growing or decreasing energies (outward-moving spiral grows, inward weakens).

Square
Earth energies (see the number four).

Star
Wish Magic, universal patterns, fulfillment.

Triangle (Upward-Facing)
Fire Element, body-mind-spirit balance.

Web
Networking.

Aromatics and Herbs

Aromatics and herbs can be brewed into your homemade candles, rubbed into prefabricated ones, placed into portable charms, or blended into potions for external application (or consumption, if edible).

Allspice
Prosperity, health, warm feelings.

Angelica
Protection.

Almond
Joy, self-control.

Apple
Harmony, health, insightfulness.

Basil
Love, peace, and safety.

Bayberry
Good fortune and abundance.

Berry (Any)
Abundance.

Borage
Bravery and improved perspectives.

Cedar
Money and cleansing.

Chamomile
Calmness, easing stress, improved sleep.

Cinnamon
Abundance, relationships.

Clove
Love.

Clover
Luck and financial improvements.

Dill
Protection (especially for children), rest.

Fennel
Banishing people or situations that bug you.

Frankincense
Bravery, luck, wealth (also good for purification).

Ginger
Energy, health, victory.

Heather
Good fortune, dedication, Weather Magic, fertility.

Honeysuckle
Intuitiveness, abundance, protection.

Jasmine
Passion, inventiveness.

Lavender
Peace, anti-stress, harmony.

Lemon
Devotion, longevity.

Marjoram
Joy.

Mint
Safety in travel, money, health.

Myrrh
Wisdom, spiritual focus, meditative aid.

Nutmeg
Psychic awareness.

Orange
Faithfulness, love.

Peach
Sagacity, joy.

Pine
Wellness, cleansing.

Rose
Devotion, love, trust.

Rosemary
Dedication, memory, love.

Sage
Wisdom and longevity.

Sandalwood
Symmetry, strength, calmness, psychic awareness.

Thyme
Bravery and communing with fairies.

Vanilla
Energy boost, improved awareness.

Timing

The ancients often used propitious timing to aid their efforts. For our purposes, the days of the week and phases of the moon and sun are the easiest things to follow for symbolic value and ease of application.

Weekdays:

Monday
White or silver (or very pale blue on a blue moon).
The best day of the week to work Candle Magic for dreaming, working through emotions, gardens, health, cleansing, fertility, Goddess-oriented efforts, and psychism.

Tuesday
Red or pink.
The best day of the week to work Candle Magic for turning away negative energy purposefully aimed at you, determination, legal matters, expansion, bravery, improved physical strength, and finances.

Wednesday
Purple.
The best day of the week to work Candle Magic for improved success in business, courage, clarity, safety abroad, the muse, and open lines of communication.

Thursday
Dark blue.
The best day of the week to work Candle Magic for love, promise-making, loyalty, divination, justice, noble ideals, commitment, and respect.

Friday
Green or yellow.
The best day of the week to work Candle Magic for developing or improving long-term relationships, kinship, personal growth, peace, passion, and social pleasure.

Saturday
Brown or black.
The best day of the week to work Candle Magic for growth, liberation, safety, tying up loose ends, banishing sadness, psychic self-defense, and the longevity of any project.

Sunday
Yellow, gold, orange.
The best day of the week to work Candle Magic for God-

oriented efforts, glamor, inventiveness, individuality, self-awareness, logic, hope, success, luck, and learning.

Moon Phases:

Blue Moon
Overcoming great obstacles, the seemingly miraculous.

Dark Moon
Weeding out unproductive habits, releasing the past, rest, secrecy.

Full Moon
Manifestation, completion, Water energies.

New Moon
Beginnings, slow but steady increase.

Waning Moon
Decrease, banishing, closure, lessening, endings.

Waxing Moon
Growth-oriented energy, increase, success, fertility.

Sun Phases:

Dawn
Inception, hope, change, increase, joy.

Noon
Blessings, energy, success, the God aspect.

Dusk
Completion, closure, endings, release.

Midnight
The Witching hour, balance, the Goddess aspect.

Seasons:

Spring
Flowering of new skills, hopefulness, friendship, gentle love, trust, overcoming negativity, change, a fresh start.

Summer
Fertility, power, strength, healing, illumination, banishing darkness, personal empowerment, and fulfillment.

Fall
Justice, harvesting what you've sown, the ongoing abundance of Earth, cleansing, conservation (frugality), balance.

Winter
The home, family, health, purification, rest, renewal, completion or closure, overcoming fear, goodwill, charity.

BIBLIOGRAPHY

Aldington, Richard, translator. *New Larousse Encyclopedia of Mythology*. Hamlyn Publishing, 1973.

Ann, Martha, et al. *Goddesses in World Mythology*. Oxford University Press, 1995.

Beyerl, Paul. *Compendium of Herbal Magick*. Phoenix Publishing, 1998.

Bruce-Mitford, Miranda. *Illustrated Book of Signs & Symbols*. DK Publishing, 1996.

Buckland, Raymond. *Advanced Candle Magic: More Spells and Rituals for Every Purpose*. Llewellyn Publications, 1996.

---. *Practical Candleburning Rituals*. Llewellyn Publications, 1970.

Budge, E. A. Wallis. *Amulets and Superstitions*. Oxford University Press, 1930.

Cavendish, Richard. *A History of Magic*. Taplinger Publishing, 1979.

Cristiani, R. S. *Perfumery and Kindred Arts: A Comprehensive Treatise on Perfumery Containing a History of Perfumes*. Henry Carey Baird & Co, 1877.

Potterton, David, editor. *Culpeper's Colour Herbal*. Sterling Publishing, 2002.

Cunningham, Scott. *Cunningham's Encyclopedia of Crystal, Gem & Metal Magic*. Llewellyn Publications, 1998.

---. *Cunningham's Encyclopedia of Magical Herbs*. Llewellyn Publications, 1985.

---. *Magic In Food: Legends, Lore & Spellwork*. Llewellyn Publications, 1991.

Davison, Michael W., editor. *Everyday Life Through the Ages.* Reader's Digest Association Ltd., 1992.

Eason, Cassandra. *Candle Power.* Cassell Illustrated, 2000.

Farrar, Jane and Stewart. *Spells and How They Work.* Phoenix Publishing Inc, 1990.

Freethy, Ron. *From Agar to Zenry: A Book of Plant Uses, Names, and Folklore.* Tanager Books, 1985.

Gordon, Leslie. *Green Magic: Flowers, Plants & Herbs in Lore & Legend.* Viking Press, 1977.

Gordon, Stuart. *Encyclopedia Myths & Legends.* Headline Book Publishing, 1993.

Hall, Manley P. *The Secret Teachings of All Ages: An Encyclopedic Outline of Masonic, Hermetic, Qabbalistic and Rosicrucian Symbolical Philosophy.* Philosophical Research Society, 1977.

Hutchinson, Ruth, et al. *Every Day's a Holiday.* Harper and Brothers, 1951.

Ketch, Tina. *Candle Lighting Encyclopedia.* 1991.

---. *Feng Shui Candle Lighting.* 1999.

Kunz, George F. *The Curious Lore of Precious Stones.* Dover Publications, 1971.

Leach, Maria, and Jerome Fried, editors. *Funk and Wagnall's Standard Dictionary of Folklore, Mythology, and Legend.* Harper & Row, 1984.

Loewe, Michael, and Carmen Blacker, editors. *Oracles and Divination.* Shambhala, 1981.

Miller, Gustavus H. *Ten Thousand Dreams Interpreted: Or What's in a Dream?* M.A. Donohue & Co, 1931.

Opie, Iona, and Moira Tatem. *A Dictionary of Superstitions.* Oxford University Press, 1989.

Oppenheimer, Betty. *The Candlemaker's Companion: A Comprehensive Guide to Rolling, Pouring, Dipping, and Decorating Your Own Candles.* Storey Books, 1997.

Telesco, Patricia. *Futuretelling.* Crossing Press, 1998.

---. *The Herbal Arts: A Handbook of Gardening, Recipes, Healing, Crafts, and Spirituality.* Crossed Crow Books, 2024.

---. *A Kitchen Witch's Cookbook.* Llewellyn Publications, 1994.

---. *Spinning Spells, Weaving Wonders: Modern Magic for Everyday Life.* Crossed Crow Books, 2024.

Walker, Barbara G. *The Woman's Dictionary of Symbols and Sacred Objects.* Harper & Row, 1988.

Waring, Philippa. *A Dictionary of Omens and Superstitions.* Chartwell Books, 1978.